'*Blend in Beautious Tints the Coloured Mass*'

Alexander Pope, *Epistle to Mr Jervas* (1716)

With best wishes

Douglas Allen

Nov 2011

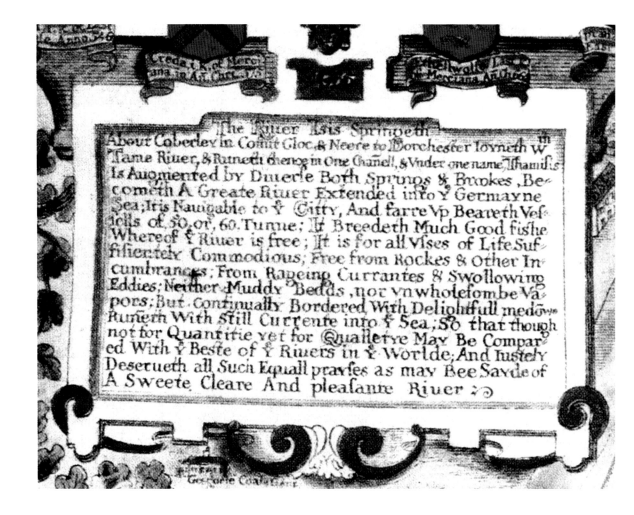

' The River Isis Springeth About Coberley in Comit[a] Gloc. & Neere to Dorchester Ioyneth w[ith] Tame River, & Runeth thence in One Chan[n]ell, & Under one name, Thamisis. Is Augmented by Diverse Both Springs & Brookes, Becometh A Greate River Extended into Y[e] Germayne Sea; It is Navigable to Y[e] Citty, And farre Up Beareth Vessells of 50 or 60 Tunne; It Breedeth Much Good fishe. Whereof Y[e] River is free; It is for all Uses of Life Sufficientely Commodious; Free from Rockes & Other Incumbrances; From Rageing Currantes & Swollowing Eddies; Neither Muddy Bedds, nor unwholesombe Vapors; But Continually Bordered With Delightfull medow[s] Run[n]eth With Still Currente into Y[e] Sea; So that though not for Quantitie yet for Qualletye May Be Compared With Y[e] Beste of Y[e] Rivers in Y[e] Worlde; And Iustely Deserveth all Such Equall prayses as may Bee Sayde of A Sweete Cleare And pleasante River. '

Moses Glover (1602–after 1635), *Isleworth Hundred being the Manor Sion and one of the Seaven Hundreds in Comita Middlesex Totally Described* (1635, illuminated parchment, detail, Syon House. Collection of the Duke of Northumberland)

David G. C. Allan

The Coloured Mass

ART AND ARTISTS
IN THE TWICKENHAM AREA
FROM TUDOR TIMES
TO THE 21ST CENTURY

Borough of Twickenham Local History Society
2011

Borough of Twickenham Local History Society Occasional Paper No. 8

Published by the Borough of Twickenham Local History Society 2011

ISBN 978-090334184-4

Designed and typeset in Monotype Plantin by Peter Moore

Printed in China
The Hanway Press Ltd, London and Lion Production

Contents

IN MEMORY OF
BRIAN LOUIS PEARCE
(1933-2006)

Sometime Librarian, Richmond upon Thames College
and Chairman, Borough of Twickenham Local History Society

Bridget Micklem (1963-)
Brian Louis Pearce, 1997
(oils, 44.5x34.5cm, private
collection)

'Tis in Pope's Grotto, and at Hampton Court
The Muse of Greater Twickenham's to be sought
She bathes at Teddington, sucks Whitton dry
And fans the flame of Bushy fountain-high.

BLP, The Fashioned Reed

Brian's Muse extended bound
Included Bushy, Whitton and much more
The Muse of Painting here is found
By Hampton's Reach and Syon's shore.

Illustrations

PART THREE : 18TH CENTURY

PART FOUR : 19TH CENTURY

PART FIVE : EARLIER 20TH CENTURY

PART SIX : LATE 20TH AND INTO THE 21ST CENTURY

EPILOGUE

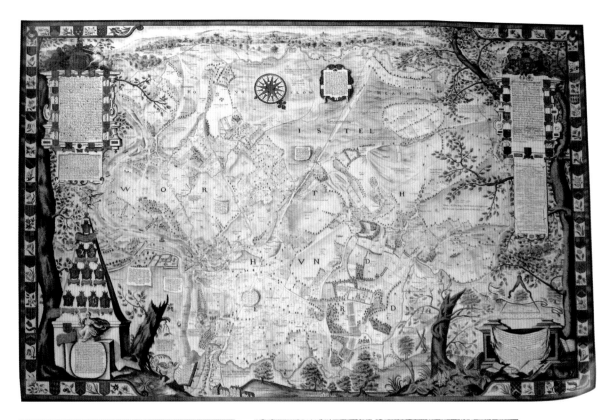

UPPER: Moses Glover (1602–after 1635), *Isleworth Hundred being the Manor Sion and one of the Seaven Hundreds in Comita Middlesex Totally Described* (1635, illuminated parchment, Syon House. Collection of the Duke of Northumberland)

LEFT: Upper cartouche from Moses Glover's map, 1635

ABOVE: Lower cartouche from Moses Glover's map, 1635

Introduction

THE GEOGRAPHICAL PROBLEM

The boundary laid down by the Borough of Twickenham Local History Society for the pursuit of its researches is, as its name implies, that of the former Borough of Twickenham. This municipality was in existence from 1926 to 1965 and was made up of the ancient parishes and manors of Hampton, Teddington, Twickenham and Whitton, which had become subject over the years to the governance of various vestries and district councils, but which 'time out of memory of man' had been contained within the Hundreds of Isleworth and Spelthorne in the County of Middlesex.[1]

Supposedly on the north bank of the river Thames, which as a 19th century observer wrote 'is here more than ordinarily tortuous',[2] the area faces north at Syon, south at Twickenham, east at Teddington and south again at Hampton. In 1965 a 'cross-river' Borough was set up, merging the Borough of Twickenham with Richmond and Kew to form the present day London Borough of Richmond upon Thames.

The study of art and artists which follows, though chiefly devoted to the area of the old Borough, will perforce include references to Richmond and Kew and to developments in Isleworth and Brentford, places which are today within the modern London Borough of Hounslow.

LIVES AND WORKS

The section on the 16th century will be concerned more with work than with lives; with the artistic creations of the Tudor dynasty and its ministers, rather than with the lives of the artists who produced them. Much is, of course, known about the artistic decoration of Hampton Court but little about James Needham, Henry VIII's Master Carpenter, who produced so much of it. His name is recorded in the list of artists at the back of this book where there will also be found the name of Hans Holbein, not because he can be considered a Twickenham artist, but because he undoubtedly visited the area. Similarly there is listed the latter-day architect of the palace, Sir Christopher Wren and the exponent of neo-classicism, Robert Adam, whose work was to extend throughout the area.

---

[1] Hampton and Teddington were added to the Borough in 1937.

[2] T. Paynter Allen, *Inquiry into the existing state of Education in Richmond, Twickenham, Mortlake and neighbourhoods*, 1870.

For the 17th century the lives of the Isleworth miniaturist Peter Oliver and of Antonio Verrio, the master of baroque splendour at Ham House, Teddington Place and Hampton Court come to the fore. The 18th century section notes the acceptance of an hierarchical theory of art, led by so called 'History' painting, followed by portraiture, landscapes, sculpture and ornament, with architecture as a combination of all these forms. Horace Walpole was conversant with this idea which was derived from the Renaissance writers whom he so much admired. Seeing himself as a latter-day Vasari he became an enthusiastic historian of art in England. Writing of Twickenham in the 1750s he boasted that it had two famous artists: Samuel Scott and Thomas Hudson.

The portraits by Hudson had much of the flair to be found in those of his pupil Reynolds. Scott's enchanting river views mark the early stage of a school of English landscape art which would embrace the great Turner in the 19th century. Turner sometimes made his landscapes 'History' paintings by giving them classical and biblical names, and Hudson and Reynolds could do the same with their portraits. The Twickenham photographers helped to replace this idea, first of all by realism, and then by atmosphere and abstraction. The 'Thames Valley' artists became a school in their own right and the 20th century saw contributions to art education, both for professionals as well as for amateurs, and to graphic and commercial art, which made the area a natural leader in these fields.

These latter-day achievements were influenced by the historical legacy of Twickenham. To practice, teach or learn art in the shadow of Sandycombe Lodge, Marble Hill, Orleans House, York House, Pope's Grotto, Strawberry Hill and Garrick's Temple was to add inspiration to creativity, enhanced by the ever-present river flowing on its curvilinear course from Hampton to Isleworth and beyond.

PART ONE : 16TH CENTURY

The Glory of God and the Splendour of Princes

THE MEDIEVAL BACKGROUND

When King Richard III, whose posthumous reputation would one day find a champion at Strawberry Hill, lost his crown to Henry Tudor in 1485, the greater part of our area was either farmland or uncultivated waste. There was at that time no naturalistic school of landscape painting but we know how the work of farming, forestry, and venery was carried on from the exquisite and detailed illustrations in the 'Books of Hours' which were so popular amongst royal and noble personages here and abroad. In these books and in the tapestries of the period, castles, abbeys and churches appear fanciful in architecture and quite out of scale, and the rivers, filled with overlarge fish and insecure craft, meander through the countryside. This is how the area would have been perceived by its humbler inhabitants, for to make a perilous voyage downstream to London, would undoubtedly require the saying of some appropriate prayer and a nod towards the great monastery of St Saviour and St Bridget, which towered about the Thames at Isleworth. Here the crafts of mason and bricklayer had been employed on the chapel and the strictly separated cloisters for the nuns and monks. Originally established by Henry V in 1415 in the rather marshy land of 'Twickenham Park', the Order had moved to what came to be called Syon in 1431 when it was richly endowed by Henry VI ('The Royal Saint'). The Brigittine sisters of Syon excelled in the arts of illumination and their wealth was augmented by their educational work amongst lay noblewomen so that by the time of the dissolution, their house was accounted one of the richest in England.

Pre-Reformation religious art in coloured glass and carved stone would also have been found in the parish churches of Isleworth (All Saints), at Twickenham and Hampton and the tiny chapel at Teddington, the last three being dedicated to Our Lady. A moated manor house at Isleworth dating from 1227 contained a stone hall with basement and kitchen and separate sleeping chambers, some reserved for the use of royalty and there was also a chapel where daily worship could be held. Walls would have been heavy with tapestries or painted cloths and ceilings coloured with stencil work. An area reserved for hunting, known variously as 'Isleworth Park' and 'The New Park of Sheen', had a large two-storied timber-framed hunting lodge built between 1375 and 1377.[1] Yet though royal and noble visitors might come to the area for transient visits and recreation it was the decision of King Henry VII to build a great palace on the south bank of the river, called, to begin with, 'Shene Palace', and then in honour of his former title, 'Richmond Palace', which led to an outpouring of Tudor magnificence in painting, gilding, carving and plasterwork which would be continued in his son's reign some four miles upstream on the Middlesex bank at Hampton Court.

HAMPTON COURT

In 1514 Thomas Wolsey, Archbishop of York and chief minister to Henry VIII, obtained a 99 year lease of the Hampton property of the knightly Order of St John. Designed and embellished by Wolsey and then by his royal master, Hampton Court Palace became a centre for artistic endeavour in the early 16th century and would again be significant in this respect in Stuart times. The Cardinal and the King employed numerous native and foreign artists and craftsmen to work at the Palace. The hammer-beam roof of the Great Hall decorated with pendants, royal arms and badges, and carved and painted heads was the work of the King's Master Carpenter James Needham (c.1532) and survives to the present day. Also extant is the ceiling (c.1535/6) of the Chapel Royal which was a replacement of the one built by Wolsey. Though made of painted wood, it simulates fan vaulting and has ribbing and pendants exquisitely decorated with heraldic motifs.

At this time the names of 'fine' artists were not generally recorded, so that although from outside sources we know that King Henry made use of the services of Hans Holbein, the list he kept of his pictures enumerates their subject matter, size and medium, but not the individuals who created them. The heraldic painters on the other hand are sometimes acknowledged by their Christian names. A rather chilling entry in the Hampton Court Accounts is of a payment made to 'Harry and John' for altering 'Queen Anne's armes unto Queen Jane's' not long after the execution of the King's second wife and his marriage to his third.[2]

After King Henry took over from Wolsey he spent more than £62,000 (the

[1]   Donald Simpson, *Twickenham Past* (London, 1993), pp.11-14.
[2]   Henry Blankston and John Hethe had previously been employed to paint and gild the Chapel ceiling. See S. Thurley, *Hampton Court: a social and architectural history* (New Haven, 2005), pp.64, 97.

equivalent of £8 million in modern money) rebuilding and remodelling Hampton Court, which it should be remembered was only one of several of great palaces either built or beautified for his use. His aim was to impress the people of England and, indeed, of the whole of Christendom. For example in August 1546 he entertained the French Ambassador and a retinue of 200 French gentlemen with their attendants, as well as 1,300 English courtiers for

Ceiling of Chapel Royal, Hampton Court, c.1535/6 (photographic detail, Hampton Court collection)

six days at Hampton Court. The Great Hall and state rooms were all put to use and outside the palace was an encampment of gold and velvet tents.

Hampton Court as created by Henry also provided a *mis-en-scène* for state occasions in his children's reigns. The boy king Edward VI gave a superb reception there for the Marshal de St André in 1551, when he was enrolled in the Order of St Michael of France. Mary I spent her honeymoon with Philip of Spain at the palace in 1554. Queen Elizabeth was regularly at Hampton Court and when the Duke of Wurtemberg came there in 1592 he called it 'the most splendid and most magnificent royal edifice to be seen in Europe'.[1]

Wenceslaus Hollar (1607-77), *View of Hampton Court*, c.1647 (drawing engraved 1780)

---

[1] S. Thurley, *Hampton Court Palace: the official guidebook* (London, 1997), p.58; S. Thurley (2005), p.80.

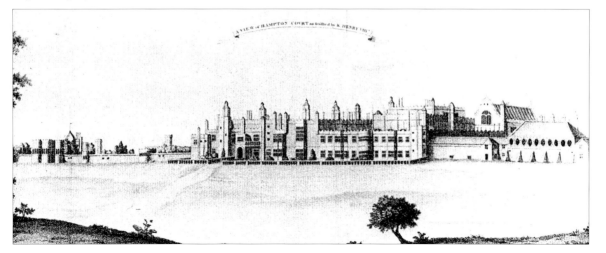

LATER TUDOR ART AND ICONOGRAPHY IN THE AREA

The magnificent funeral cortege of King Henry VIII (d.1547) halted for a night at the former monastery of Syon on the way from Westminster to Windsor. The boy King Edward VI (1547-53) was crowned soon afterwards and his uncle Edward Seymour, Duke of Somerset, and Protector of the Realm, employed masons and gardeners to transform Syon into a quasi-royal palace. A quadrangular structure of white stone with a turret at each angle and flat leaden roofs disguised by ornamental crenellation was built around a courtyard of 80 square feet. The east and west fronts had gardens enclosed in high walls for the sake of privacy, but between them the Duke raised a triangular terrace from where he could view the surrounding countryside. His enemies called this a 'fortification' and accused him at the time of his attainder of wishing to tyrannise over England from this stronghold by the Thames. His successor John Dudley, Duke of Northumberland, then seized the property and held it until his fall at the succession of Queen Mary I (1553-58). The Brigittine Sisters then briefly returned before being expelled again, this time more peacefully, by Queen Elizabeth I (1558-1603) who eventually granted the property to Henry Percy, 9th Earl of Northumberland (1564-1632) who in the next century would employ Inigo Jones to 'new front' the inner court and finish the Great Hall.

Earlier in Elizabeth's reign a large timber framed mansion, with lower courses of brick, was built in Twickenham Park (1561/62). This has been called the first large secular residence, apart from Hampton Court and Syon Park House to be built in the area, though it was presumably ante-dated by the stone 13th century Manor House already mentioned and the Twickenham Manor House in Church Street, known to have been built of early 16th century bricks, and traditionally associated with Catherine of Aragon.[1]

One of Queen Elizabeth's favourites, the lawyer, scientist and essayist, Francis Bacon, Lord Verulam lived at Twickenham Park from about 1580 to 1608 and created a celebrated garden. 'The situation of that place' he said was 'much convenient for the trial of my philosophical experiments'. Less well known Twickenham Elizabethans were Vincent Pointer, 'a most cunning grafter and planter of all manner of rare fruits' and a Mr Craston who planted nurseries and orchards just east of the manor house and St Mary's Church.[2]

This parish church, like all the others in the area, would have all been deprived of its medieval decoration by 1561, though in the Royal chapels at Richmond and Hampton Court the Queen would maintain the colour and richness of pre-Reformation times.[3]

---

[1] Simpson (1993), p.53.   [2] Ibid, pp.31, 60, 116.

[3] A. Beckles Willson, *The Church of St Mary the Virgin, Twickenham* (Twickenham, 2000), pp.39-46.

When at Hampton Court the Queen showed the reverence which both her brother and her sister had felt for their father's work. In the 1560s she ordered the enrichment of a 'privy chamber' and the building of a 'privy kitchen'. A bay window inscribed 1568 can still be seen from the pond gardens. In 1584 a fountain of marble was acquired. This has now gone but the set of five Flemish tapestries brought by the Queen and showing scenes from Virgil's *Aeneid* depicting *Dido and Aeneas* are still at the Palace. Otherwise the building and grounds stood much as King Henry had left them.[1]

The Elizabethan court was constantly on the move. Within a ten mile radius of London the Queen journeyed about from Whitehall, to Greenwich, to Windsor, to Richmond and to Hampton Court. She could be seen, wrote Sir John Neale, in his classic biography 'like some very human and approachable goddess with her train, going by river or road from one of these palaces to another, or visiting other royal houses or private homes in the near neighbourhood of London'.

In high summer she would go farther afield on her slow and stately progresses into distant counties, but always returning by the autumn to keep Christmas at Whitehall followed by a New Year's return to Hampton Court. In 1584 as public fears of Spanish and Jesuitical assassination plots spread throughout the land, throngs of people watched her journey to Hampton 'kneeling on the ground they wished her a thousand blessings, and prayed that those who meant her harm might be discovered and punished as they deserved'.[2]

[1]   Thurley (1997), pp.9, 59; Thurley (2000), p.87.

[2]   J.E.Neale, *Queen Elizabeth* (London, 1934), pp. 205, 265.

Andrea Mantegna (c.1431-1506), *The Triumph of Caesar VI*, c.1500
(tempera on canvas, 268 x 278 cm, Hampton Court.
The Royal Collection, © 2010 Her Majesty Queen Elizabeth II)

PART TWO : 17TH CENTURY

Masters of the Baroque

THE ROYAL STUART CONNECTION

About two o'clock on the morning of 24 March 1603 at Richmond Palace the great Queen breathed her last. Sir Robert Carey set off on his historic ride to Scotland, which ended on the evening of the 27th when he knelt before King James and 'saluted him by his title of England, Scotland, France and Ireland'. Thus began a reign in which the polymath Inigo Jones, already mentioned in connection with his work at Syon, brought the arts of architecture, scene painting and garden design into an extraordinary harmony, and the school of English miniature painting which had begun to flower at the Queen's court reached a high level of perfection.

The Oliver family of miniaturists or 'limners', as they were called at the time, came to have local connections. Isaac Oliver (c.1565-1617) had been brought as a child to England in 1568 when his Huguenot parents fled from Rouen. Isaac's skill as a miniaturist is shown in a self portrait he painted in the mid 1590s. It was acquired in the 18th century by Horace Walpole who said of it 'The art of the master and the imitation of nature are so great in it that the largest magnifying glass only calls out new beauties'. Isaac Oliver learnt the art of 'limning' under the great Elizabethan miniaturist Nicholas Hilliard (1547-1619) one of whose financial ventures was a metalworks by

Isaac Oliver (c.1565-1617),
Self portrait, miniature, c.1590
(engraved by J.S. Müller, 1712)

the river at Isleworth. By the time of King James's accession Isaac had an established practice at Austin Friars in London and by 1604 had become limner to Queen Anne (the Queen Consort) and been attached to the household of Prince Henry (heir to the throne until his death in 1612) at Richmond Palace. In 1606 Isaac Oliver married Elizabeth Harding (his third wife) at All Saints Church, Isleworth.

His son by his first wife, Peter Oliver (c.1594-1646), also a miniaturist of genius, prospered under the patronage of Prince Henry's younger brother Charles, and was employed after Prince Charles became King to make exquisite miniature copies of the Italian, Flemish and French masterpieces in the ever-expanding royal collection. When not at court Peter Oliver sought refuge at a property in Isleworth where he had as a neighbour Moses Glover (b.1601), the artist cartographer who produced the famous map of the area in 1635 (see p.14). Moses Glover worked as a freeman of the Painter Stainers Company in the City of London and also practised at Isleworth. He married the widow of Richard Guthrie, an Isleworth painter, in 1626.

Peter Oliver (c.1594-1647), *Self portrait in profile to the left*, c.1630 (miniature, graphite and watercolour on card, 8.6 x 6.7cm)

It cannot have been a happy marriage since his wife was twice had up for being a 'common scold' and on the second occasion was sentenced to be publicly ducked. We may imagine him as being glad to spend time travelling around the area to produce his map, which as well as showing the geographical features and built environment, also named the owners and residents of properties, and thus took the form of a census.[1]

King James's court followed the peripatetic pattern set by Elizabeth, except that the new King spent at least a third of each year hunting hares and deer, when the courtiers and their ladies endured great discomfort and expense in hard to come by lodgings in the little towns of Royston or Newmarket or in unheated portable pavilions. The royal palaces were of course also visited at different times of the year, the end of September being the times for the establishment of what was called 'a standing court' at Hampton Court. Though lords and ladies might be lodged within the overcrowded Palace, their servants had to find shelter amidst rows of brightly painted temporary tents put up to house the menials serving in the royal kitchens and stables. The King like Elizabeth made no drastic changes to the appearance of the Palace and we may imagine that he looked upon it from

[1] See *ODNB* under Moses Glover, Isaac and Peter Oliver; and the account of the Oliver family in *Walpole Society* vol. v, 1978/80, pp.75-86.

the start of his reign as yet one more example of the unbelievable magnificence which was now his to enjoy after the years of penny-pinching in Scotland.

Using it for his famous conference on the Church settlement in 1604 and for numerous state ceremonies over the years, he would have had on display the regularly commissioned portraits of himself and his family by Mytens and van Somer, examples of which can now be seen at Windsor and Syon.[1]

After Francis Bacon left Twickenham Park the house was rebuilt in 1608/9 on the lines of the Jacobean mansion soon to be built on the Surrey side of the river at Ham. It was first occupied by Lucy, Countess of Bedford (c.1581-1627) the close friend of the Queen Consort. The Countess remained in possession until 1617 enlarging Bacon's gardens and pleasure grounds and giving hospitality to poets, artists as well as courtiers. Later 17th and 18th century occupants continued the work of landscape gardening, employing among others Daniel Langley and his more famous son Batty Langley (1696-1751) between 1702 and 1727. Although the house was demolished in 1803 and the grounds were encircled by villas in the 1860s, several tall plane trees planted by Batty Langley survive to this day.[2]

Encouraged by his mother and his short-lived elder brother Henry, Prince Charles had developed an interest in the arts at an early age. Described by Rubens as '*le prince le plus amateur de la peinture qui soit au monde*', Charles, once he became King in 1625, would use the royal palaces as galleries for the display of his collection of old and modern masterpieces. At Hampton Court he found room for one of his most famous acquisitions, the *Triumph of Caesar*, a sequence of nine paintings by Andrea Mantegna which had been painted c.1485-1505 at Mantua in Italy for the Ducal Family of Gonzaga (see p.22). The King purchased the paintings in 1629 and had them hung at Hampton Court in the following year. He also paid for new works such as Artemisia Gentileschi's *Self portrait* which has been dated at c.1630.

Though following his predecessors' practice of maintaining the Henrician ambience of the palace, Charles I had there over 350 easel paintings in contrast to Henry VIII who had fewer than 50. Before the calamities which overtook him in the latter part of his reign he further enriched the interior of the Chapel and beautified the Privy garden where he employed the Florentine sculptor Francesco Fanelli (fl.1608-65) to create a statue of Arethusa, today known as the 'Diana Fountain' and to be seen in Bushy Park.[3] Resident briefly in 1647,

---

[1]   Thurley (1997) p.65; G.P.V. Akrigg, *Jacobean Pageant at the Court of King James* (London, 1962), pp.151-6.

[2]   Simpson (1993), pp.14-5; 60-1, 84, 127.

[3]   M. Whinney and Ol. Millar, *English Art 1625-1774* (Oxford, 1957), p.122; Thurley (2004) p.145.

LEFT: Artemisia Gentileschi (1593-1652/53), *Self portrait*, c.1630 (oils, 195 x 62 cm. The Royal Collection, © 2010 Her Majesty Queen Elizabeth II)

RIGHT: Sir Peter Lely (1618-80), *Charles I and James, Duke of York*, 1647 (oils, Syon House. Collection of the Duke of Northumberland)

though treated as King, he was *de facto* a prisoner of Cromwell's army, which in 1649 would bring about his death. Before this the Puritan zealots had already begun to sell off the major part of the King's collection. Cromwell, who would himself live at the Palace from 1654 to 1658, retained the Mantegna *Triumph* and the Raphael cartoons showing the Acts of the Apostles. 'The first' it has been suggested 'appealed to his military, the second to his evangelical mind.'[1]

It was during the King's sojourn at Hampton Court in 1647 that the newly arrived Dutch painter Peter Lely (1617-80) was commissioned by the Earl of Northumberland, the guardian of the royal children at Syon, to paint the evocative *Charles I with James, Duke of York*, still to be seen at Syon. Lely went on to have a successful private practice under the Cromwellian regime and an outstanding career as royal portrait painter to King Charles II, culminating with the honour of Knighthood on 11 January 1680, some ten months before his death.

'SIGNIOR VERRIO'

At the Restoration Hampton Court reverted to the crown and in October 1660 Charles II, only six months after his return to England, began to renovate the structure. He set up some of his father's pictures which had survived the great sale of 1648, he rearranged those retained by Cromwell and made new additions

[1] R. Bishop, *Paintings of the Royal Collection* (London, 1937), p.20.

to the collection. He tracked down Anne Oliver at Isleworth and purchased from her by means of an annuity an important set of her late husband's miniatures. In 1662 Charles bought 72 paintings from Dutch art dealers and dispatched 18 of them to Hampton Court. This was the year of Samuel Pepys' first visit, a day's outing recorded with characteristic verve in his diary for 12 May. A 4am start on a journey by barge to Mortlake, by foot to Richmond, by boat from Richmond to Teddington, and by foot from Teddington to the palace, culminated in a tour of the whole property, 'which indeed is nobly furnished, particularly the Queen's (Catherine of Braganza) bed, given her by the States of Holland. A looking glass sent by the Queen Mother (Henrietta Maria) from France, hanging in the Queen's chamber. And many brave pictures.'[1]

In the same year, 1662, the King employed André Mollet to lay out the Great Avenue and 'Great Canal or Long Water' in the Home Park beyond the east front of the Palace. Later in his reign a house for the Duke of York was built in the grounds and a set of lodgings for Lady Castlemaine added to the south east corner of the Palace, both in a contemporary or 'Wren' style. Although the King's main interests were centred on the new state rooms and the park at Windsor where his much favoured artist Antonio Verrio (c.1639-1707) was given *carte blanche*, he appears to have sought Verrio's advice on garden design as well as on painted decoration for Hampton Court.

Born c.1639 in the Kingdom of Naples, Antonio Verrio had been encouraged to pursue an artistic career by his family from an early age. As well as painting religious subjects for the Jesuit College in Naples, he worked for a time in Florence, Rome and Genoa. Moving to France in the mid 1660s he lived first in Toulouse and then in 1671 in Paris. Elected a member of the Académie Royale de Peinture, he worked at Versailles under Charles Le Brun where he mastered the rich baroque style for which he would become famous in England. Coming to London in 1672 with the Duke

Antonio Verrio (1639-1707), *Self portrait* , c.1688-98 (oils, The Burghley House Collection)

---

1 *Walpole Society Volume*; loc.cit; R. Latham and W. Matthews, eds., *The Diary of Samuel Pepys* (London, 1970-83) entry for 12 May 1662; Thurley (2000), pp.133, 147.

of Montagu as his patron, he was appointed by the King as a designer for the newly revived Mortlake Tapestry works in 1674. In this year he painted a flamboyant *Sea Triumph* which is now held at Hampton Court and which would be echoed in his work in the Great Hall at Chelsea Hospital. His success was now assured and apart from those from the King and his brother he received commissions from Lord Arlington, the Duke of Monmouth, Sir Stephen Fox, Nell Gwynne, the Earl of Essex, the Earl of Exeter and the Duke and Duchess of Lauderdale. His work for the Lauderdales at Ham House shows his skill at baroque imagery used on a small scale. His painting for Christ's Hospital, now at Horsham in Sussex, is said to be the largest work on canvas ever undertaken. The story of his witty exchanges with Charles II and for his insistence on being called 'Signior' passed into legend. Shorn of his royal posts by the Revolution and with his son following the Jacobite cause in Ireland, he was given generous hospitality by Lord Exeter at Burghley House in Lincolnshire, where the so called 'Heaven Room' still astounds visitors as it once did Horace Walpole. Back to the South in 1700 Verrio decorated Teddington Place for Sir Charles Duncombe with ceilings depicting *Jupiter descending in a shower of gold to Danäe* and a scene on Mount Olympus which clearly owed much to his work at Burghley. Teddington Place has not survived but the private dining room of William of Orange at Hampton Court which Verrio also decorated in 1700 remains on view.[1]

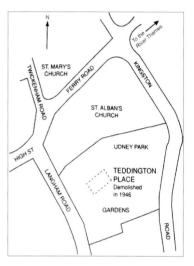

Plan of Udney Park Gardens, Teddington

The private dining room was situated by the river away from the main structure of the Palace. Soon William would employ the architectural polymath Sir Christopher Wren to transform the south and east side of the Palace. During his work at Hampton Court Wren often stayed in a house outside the palace, but Verrio, under special royal protection and exempt from the anti-catholic laws, was given a set of rooms by the Tudor gateway.

In 1701 just before William's death, Verrio began his work on the newly built staircase hall leading to the King's apartment. His flying *putti* and reclining deities carry the eye upwards to a *trompe l'oeil* sky on the ceiling where the apotheosis of the House of Orange is represented. It is an extraordinarily audacious composition and the wall which shows the Emperor Julian writing at Mercury's dictation has been praised for its dignity and spaciousness, though

---

[1]   E. Croft-Murray, *Decorative Painting in England 1537-1837*, Vol. 1 (London 1962), pp. 50-60. Information supplied by Mrs C. Brett.

Antonio Verrio (1639-1707), *The King's staircase, Hampton Court* (photograph, Hampton Court collection)

critics have been hard on the over-intensity of the colours. Verrio's final work was the Queen's Drawing Room (1702-4) in which Queen Anne and her Consort, Prince George of Denmark, Lord High Admiral, are celebrated and British Sea Power is glorified in an illusionist temple supported by pink marble pilasters.

Queen Anne allowed the painter to stay out the rest of his days at the Palace. He died on 15 June 1707 having made a will two days before, in which he made bequests to his two sons, and to his grandson and granddaughter. He was buried at the Hampton parish church of St Mary's, probably in the vaults, but without a memorial. His influence, via his sometime assistants, Thornhill and Laguerre, could be seen in the dome ceiling at St Paul's and the 'Painted Hall' at Greenwich. Pope helped to immortalise him in the oft-repeated lines:

> On painted Ceilings you devoutly stare
> Where sprawl the Saints of *Verrio* or *Laguerre*
> On gilded clouds in fair expansion lie
> And bring all Paradise before your Eye.[1]

An English craftsman who unlike Verrio does have a memorial at St Mary's Hampton is Huntingdon Shaw (1659-1710). Shaw, it seems, rather than Verrio's compatriot Jean Tijou, deserves the credit for the famous garden screen at Hampton Court. His tombstone carries the inscription:

> He was an artist in his way
> He designed and executed
> The Ornamental Ironwork at Hampton Court Palace.[2]

SIR GODFREY KNELLER

Like Verrio, Sir Godfrey Kneller was a naturalised foreigner who from his arrival in England in the 1670s until his death in 1723 was perfectly at ease in his adopted country. He painted several portraits of Charles II and in the next reign produced state portraits of James II and Mary of Modena. After the Revolution he was appointed 'Principal Painter' to William III and Mary II, and was knighted in 1692; in due course he painted – with the help of assistants – multiple portraits of successive sovereigns and their consorts from Queen Anne to George II. He was the first artist to enjoy the status of a country gentleman. In 1709 he purchased a house and estate in the centre of Whitton. He demolished the existing partly medieval building

Sir Godfrey Kneller (1646-1723), *Self portrait*, c.1706-1711 (engraved by J. Faber, 1735. Author's collection)

[1] A. Pope, *Epistle to the Rt Hon Richard, Earl of Burlington* (1731); Croft Murray (1962), pp.59-60; information supplied by Mr J. C. Sheaf.

[2] Transcription supplied by Mrs Joan Heath.

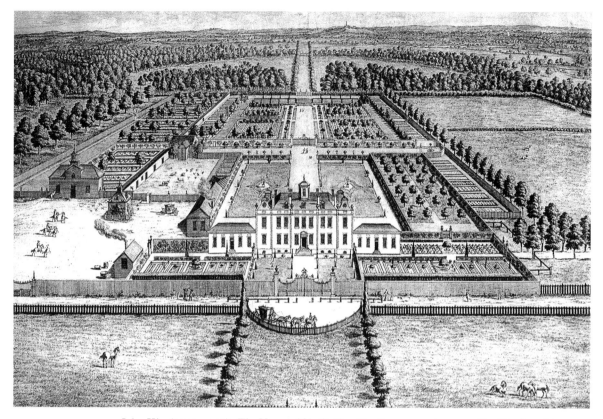

John Kip (1653-1722), *The House of Sir Godfrey Kneller*, c.1715 (engraved by Kip from his drawing)

and replaced it with a magnificent baroque residence, set in extensive ornamental grounds and approached by long avenues. Inside there was a hall and staircase decorated to Kneller's design by Verrio's talented assistant, Louis Laguerre (1663-1723) in the established illusionist manner, with Kneller himself helping with the paintwork. Sir Godfrey served as a churchwarden at St Mary's Church, Twickenham from 1713 to 1717, and was involved in fund raising for a new nave and chancel following the structural collapse of 1713.[1]

Kneller's social aspirations were laughed at by many of his contemporaries and Alexander Pope went so far as to say, after the artist's death, 'Sir Godfrey was very covetous...very vain and a great glutton'. Yet the poet had always admired his talents as a painter and composed an epitaph 'Imitated from the famous Epitaph on Raphael' which was inscribed on Kneller's monument in Westminster Abbey. Kneller had intended that another monument should be erected at St Mary's after the burial of his remains in a family vault he had constructed at his own charge below the north wall of the new nave. He designed an immense

---

[1] Simpson (1993), p.62; M. Whinney and O. Millar, (1957), p.195; *ODNB* under Godfrey Kneller.

baroque confection which would have rivalled the grand structures put up to Thomas Harvie in 1693 by John Bushnell and moved to a central position in the rebuilt nave. At Hampton in the 1730s Thomas Archer's 'Thomas' memorial would display a similarly extravagant mixture of classical allegory and family pride.

Kneller had hoped that Pope would allow the monument to replace the memorial erected to the poet's father, but Pope demurred and an unseemly lawsuit with Lady Kneller ensued. People were relieved when it was decided that the intended memorial was on too large a scale to be supported by the fabric of the church. Kneller is today commemorated by a stained glass panel on the north wall of the church.[1] Another and far less famous portrait painter, Edward Seymour, who lived in Twickenham from at least 1722 onwards was buried in the churchyard in 1759. But this takes our story well into the 18th century when, as Horace Walpole put

Thomas Archer (c.1668-1743), *Thomas Memorial*, St Mary's Hampton, 1731 (photograph: Peter Moore)

it, Twickenham had 'many famous people' among whom he listed the painter Thomas Hudson, who settled at Cross Deep in 1753 near to what had become something of a national memorial, the villa and grotto of 'Alexander Pope Esq Deceased'.

---

[1]　M.R. Brownell, *Alexander Pope and the Arts of Georgian England* (Oxford, 1978), pp.23-4, 351-2; Anthony Beckles Willson (2000), pp.19, 26. Further information supplied by Mr Beckles Willson.

PART THREE : 18TH CENTURY

Connoisseurship and 'High Art' versus Portraiture

THE POPE CIRCLE

Alexander Pope's riverside villa at Cross Deep with its famous grotto and gardens acted as a magnet for artists of all sorts. Pope had in his youth studied painting in the London studio of Charles Jervas (c.1695-1739) and acquired the ability to sketch figures and copy old and modern masters which he applied later to landscape design and architecture. When Jervas, who in spite of Kneller's low opinion of his talents prospered as a portrait painter, acquired a house at Hampton, Pope 'laid out' a garden for him based on the Twickenham model.[1]

[1]   Brownell (1978), p.148.

Alexander Pope (1688-1744), *View of Twickenham Church from his garden*, n.d. (pencil sketch in the flyleaf of his copy of *Homeri Opera*, vol. I, 1707, Lewis Walpole collection, Yale University)

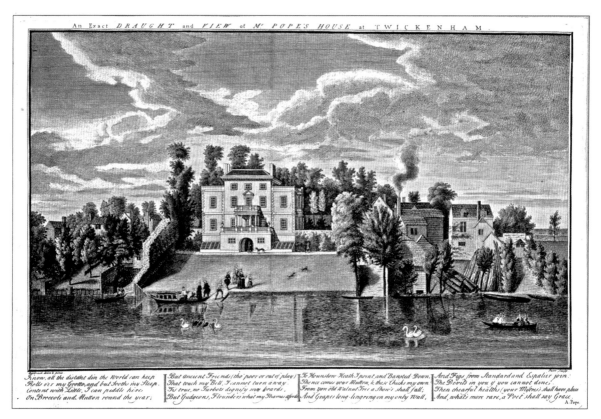

An Exact *DRAUGHT* and *VIEW* of M.r *POPE'S HOUSE* at TWICKENHAM.

Peter Rysbrack (1690-1748), *Mr Pope's House at Twickenham* (engraved by N. Parr, c.1735, Richmond Borough Art Collection, Orleans House Gallery)

Thomas Hudson (1701-79), another prosperous portrait painter, came to Twickenham a few years after Pope's death. He purchased a riverside site not far from Pope's Villa and like Pope extended his property to the other side of the highway. Facing the river Hudson built a miniature rusticated Palladian villa of two stories with projecting end bays each having pedimented attic pavilions joined by a stone balustrade, where he housed his collection of Italian masters, acquired on his recently completed 'Grand Tour'. Beneath the highway he had a tunnel dug for access to a second villa, which appears to have been made out of an older property to which Hudson gave a 'stage Gothic' façade. Horace Walpole, who admired Hudson as an artist, would not have liked this attempt at an architectural style of which he would become the master, preferring an asymmetrical and more scholarly interpretation, which the landscape artist Paul Sandby (1725-1808) was to illustrate so well in his several views of Strawberry Hill (see p.41).[1]

Hudson's close friend and sometime neighbour was the landscape artist Samuel Scott (1710-72) who, after living for a short time by the river, took a sub-lease

[1]   A. Beckles Willson, *Strawberry Hill and history of the New House* (London, 1998), passim; *Mr Pope and others at Cross Deep Twickenham in the 18th century* (London, 1996), pp.109-115.

Samuel Scott (c.1710-72), *Twickenham on the Thames*, 1760 (oils, Richmond Borough Art Collection, Orleans House Gallery)

of part of Twickenham Manor House in Church Street. Known as 'the English Canaletto', Scott drew and painted a number of Twickenham views, notably of 'Riverside', of Pope's Villa, of Radnor House, of 'Cross Deep', and of St Mary's Church as seen from the first floor windows of the Manor House. Scott left Twickenham in 1765 but his equally talented pupil, William Marlow (1740-1813), famous for his river views, lived at the Manor House from 1775 to 1813, sharing it towards the end of his life in what was rumoured to be a *ménage à trois* with John Curtis (fl.1790-1822) and his wife. Curtis was also an artist and

had been Marlow's pupil. He exhibited at the Royal Academy until 1822 but never achieved the success of either Scott or Marlow.[1]

However much it might have been desired by Pope's circle, the establishment of a Royal Academy of Arts would have to wait until the reign of George III.

William Marlow (1740-1813), *The Thames at Twickenham*, c.1808 (pencil and pen & ink, from a sketchbook, Tate Gallery)

[1]   Simpson (1993), pp.35, 55.

Joshua Gosselin
(1739-1813),
*Whitton Dean near
Hounslow*, 1791
(watercolour,
private collection)

HANOVERIAN PATRONAGE

The first two Kings of the House of Hanover were not generally regarded as either collectors or patrons of art in this country though both beautified and extended their palace at Herrenhausen in their native land. In England George I sat, as of necessity, for his portraits by Kneller, and kept royal state at Hampton Court where he ordered the completion of Queen Anne's decorative schemes. His son, George Louis, Prince of Wales, for whom he felt a pathological jealousy, also stayed at the Palace until he was barred from the royal residences in 1717. Ten years later George Louis succeeded to the crown, by which time he had built up some local connections through the Argyll family at Whitton and at his

Augustin Heckel
(c.1690-1770),
*The Countess of
Suffolk's House*
[Marble Hill
House], 1748
(oils, Richmond
Borough Art
Collection,
Orleans House
Gallery)

John Boydell
(1719-1804), *The
Thames between
Richmond and
Isleworth*, c.1755.
(engraving,
Richmond
Borough Art
Collection,
Orleans House
Gallery)

residences at Richmond. As Prince of Wales he was entertained at the famous
Twickenham Octagon belonging to James Johnston, Secretary of State for
Scotland. Subsequent to his accession as King he employed the Twickenham
builder/architect, Roger Morris (1649-1759) at the White Lodge in Richmond
Park and settled his mistress Henrietta Howard, the gifted friend of Pope and
the artist Charles Jervas, at Marble Hill (c.1728/29) which was another of
Roger Morris's 'Palladian' buildings. George's ever-tolerant Queen, Caroline
of Ansbach, enjoyed embellishing the semi-palatial Richmond Lodge which
her husband linked to the White Lodge by a private road. She visited the
Twickenham Octagon in 1729.

Unlike her husband, who was impervious to any art except music and who had
declared his dislike of 'boets' and 'bainters', the Queen could distinguish between
good and bad in the royal collection and tried in vain to get the King to bring
back the Van Dycks into prominence. Yet it was their eldest son, Frederick, Prince
of Wales, for whom they had a shared dislike, who had the greatest knowledge of
and appreciation of that collection. The well known family row of 1737 brought
to an end the use of Hampton Court as a sovereign's residence. Frederick would
in future make Kew the jumping-off place for his many encounters with Pope
and his circle. In due course his own son the future George III inherited both an
attachment to Kew and an interest in the arts.[1]

Frederick had always sympathised with those patrons and artists who would
have liked to see the establishment in England of an Academy or Society similar to those which flourished in France and Italy. Before his unexpected death
in 1751 he had approved a scheme to give prizes to young artists of promise,
though he had admitted that 'his Finances would not bear such a burden which
was fitter for his Royal Father's encouragement'. The close-fisted George II
gave no support to the 'Society for the encouragement of Arts, Manufactures

---

[1] Beckles Willson (1996), passim; Simpson (1993), 26, 37, 41, 44, 64; R. Halsband, *Lord
Hervey* (Oxford, 1973), pp.186-7.

and Commerce' (now the RSA) when it was founded in 1754. Fortunately the far from wealthy art teacher and philanthropist William Shipley (1715-1803) who had projected the scheme, was given an introduction to the Revd Dr Stephen Hales FRS (1677-1761), parish priest of Teddington, and through Hales received the backing of two influential noblemen and of a wealthy local tradesman.

(studio of) Thomas Hudson (1701-79), *Stephen Hales, DD, FRS*, c.1759 (engraved from the oil painting)

Hales, who had been frequently visited by the late Prince, now held the office of Chaplain to his widow, the Dowager princess Augusta of Wales, who sought his advice on the development of her botanical collection at Kew, and allowed him a share in the upbringing of her children. On one occasion Hales helped the Royal household with making landscape pictures from sea mosses.[1]

As a founder and Vice-President of the Society of Arts Stephen Hales lived to see several artists and patrons who were either residents or who had local connections elected as members: Dr Charles Morton, British Museum curator, and Joshua Reynolds in 1756; Sir William Chambers and Matthew Duane, connoisseur friend to Horace Walpole, in 1757; David Garrick in 1758; and the Earl of Bute and Thomas Hudson in 1761. The Society's prize winners in Hales's time included Simon Taylor (c.1748-96) in 1756 and 1760, and William Pars (1714-82) in 1756 and 1757. Taylor became a successful botanical painter, being engaged by Lord Bute to illustrate the plants at Kew. Pars would be employed by Horace Walpole to draw his *View of Richmond Hill, Twickenham and Mr Pope's House from the terrace of Strawberry Hill*. William Woollett (1735-85) who had drawn and engraved views of Whitton Park in 1757 won a prize for older artists in 1759. The young amateur Lady Louisa Augusta Greville won honorary prizes in 1758, 1759 and 1760. Horace Walpole (elected a member in 1762) thought highly of her work and had some examples in his collection at Strawberry Hill.[2]

In 1760 the Society of Arts had held in its newly built 'Great Room' designed by Sir William Chambers, the first exhibition of modern British art. Works by Cosway, Pars and Reynolds and Roubiliac's model for his statue of Shakespeare

[1] D.G.C. Allan, *William Shipley* (London, 1979), p.17; (with R.E. Schofield) *Stephen Hales* (London, 1980), p.115; BOTLHS *Paper 69*, pp. 5-6.

[2] BOTLHS *Paper 69*, pp.7-10. Information supplied by Mrs Pat Francis.

Sir Joshua Reynolds (1723-1792), *The Thames from Richmond Hill*, 1788 (oils, Tate Gallery)

and Hayman's portrait of *Garrick as Richard III* were on show and Horace Walpole was among the visitors. During the next eight years the artists, having quarrelled first with the Society itself, began to form equally quarrelsome institutions of their own. Eventually William Chambers sought an audience with the King and on 28 November 1768 His Majesty promised to give his 'patronage, protection and support' to Chambers' scheme for a combined teaching and exhibiting institution. On 10 December the King signed 'the Instrument of Foundation' and the Royal Academy came into being with Reynolds as President and Chambers as Treasurer. The designatory letters ARA and RA would soon become honours coveted by British artists, equivalent as Reynolds put to 'a title of nobility'.[1]

Reynolds had stayed in the area on several occasions before he finally commissioned William Chambers to build him a country retreat known as the 'Wick' on Richmond Hill, prompting the famous exchange with his old master Hudson,

---

[1] S. Hutchison, *The Royal Academy of Arts 1768-1968* (London, 1968), passim; H. Hoock, *The King's Artists* (Oxford, 2003), passim.

who, thinking of the days when the celebrated President of the Academy was his pupil, commented: 'Little did I think we should ever have country seats opposite each other'. To which Reynolds is said to have replied: 'Little did I think when I was a young man, that I should look down on Mr Hudson.'[1]

Reynolds would have called on Chambers at Whitton Place, which the celebrated architect had leased in 1767, and was frequently at Richard Owen Cambridge's villa on the site of what is now called Cambridge Park. There is a rare surviving landscape by Reynolds showing the view from Richmond Hill of the Thames winding its way through Twickenham and past Pope's villa. Reynolds' many commissions from Horace Walpole were most likely done in London, though his *Out of Town Party* (1761) suggests from its title that it was painted at Strawberry Hill.[2]

Sir Joshua Reynolds (1723-1792), *The Out of Town Party*, 1759-61 (oils, City Art Gallery, Bristol)

STRAWBERRY HILL

Horace Walpole, whose name has already figured in our pages, was at once patron of living artists, collector of historic artefacts and an amateur designer of remarkable discrimination and taste. His famous father had ensured for him the means to please himself as to a place of residence. At the age of 30, with the experience of a 'Grand Tour' and service in Parliament behind him he sought a retreat from his town house in Arlington Street and settled on Strawberry Hill, Twickenham: a cottage set in five acres midway between Pope's villa and Teddington. It was not really a hill, but the land sloped from a height of 33' towards the River Thames 'in enamelled meadows, with filigree hedges'. As for the 'strawberries' no gloss has been given for the name, but Walpole did not hesitate to adopt it, perhaps with Ducal thoughts or because of Richard III's ominous request to the Bishop of Ely. By 1749 he was calling his 'little rural bijoux' *Strawberry Castle*, and after two years of experiment with architectural styles he settled on the 'Gothick' and began to create the extraordinary structure – half abbey and half baronial hall, which by the 1780s had become a Twickenham 'sight', open to visitors in the manner of a modern National Trust or English Heritage property.[3]

[1]   Simpson (1993), p.35.   [2]   Simpson (1993), p.64; BOTLHS *Paper 69*, p.6.

[3]   W.S. Lewis, *Horace Walpole* (London, 1961), pp.101, 129-31.

Paul Sandby (1725-1808), *South view of Strawberry Hill*, c.1779 (oils, Richmond Borough Art Collection, Orleans House Gallery)

Walpole even had a guide printed for visitors, who were shown round by his servants. On display were Greek and Roman bronzes, intaglios, medals and coins, medieval English coins, enamels and glass, the miniatures by Isaac and Peter Oliver and Nicholas Hilliard, and drawings by Hans Holbein. Twelve thousand portrait prints and drawings could be examined in portfolios. Hanging on the walls were framed oil paintings of Henry VII and Henry VIII and a complete set of Hogarth's engravings as well as the artist's *Sarah Malcolm* and a sketch of *The Beggar's Opera*. A portrait by George Romney entitled *Lady Craven* had a special interest, since the sitter later married a German Prince, and made a prize winning image of her royal husband.[1]

John Henry Muntz (fl.1755-75), *Horace Walpole in his library*, c.1770 (engraving of watercolour, Lewis Walpole collection, Yale University)

[1]   BOTLHS *Paper 74* (1997), pp.18-19.

Sir Joshua Reynolds (1723-92),
The Three Ladies Waldegrave, 1780
(oils, National Gallery of Scotland.
Lady Laura in the centre)

Guiseppe Ceracchi
(c.1751-1801),
Anne Seymour Damer,
c.1780 (life size
statue, © Trusteees of
the British Museum)

Richard
Cosway (1742-1821),
Mrs Damer, c.1790
(engraved from a
drawing formerly at
Strawberry Hill)

Contemporary artists who worked at Strawberry Hill included William Pars and Richard Cosway already mentioned. Johann Heinrich Muntz (fl.1755-1775) a Swiss expert on encaustic colouring, had the title of 'Resident Artist', Reynolds may have visited the house to paint Walpole's talented great-nieces, *The Ladies Waldegrave* and Ozias Humphry also came there to paint them. The line between amateur and professional was not strictly drawn. Lady Laura Waldegrave had won the Society of Arts gold medal in 1779 for her drawings and the same award went to Lady Caroline Walpole in 1780, who also won a silver medal in 1781. Horace kept examples of their work, with those of Lady Louisa Greville, in a special portfolio. The sculptress Anne Seymour Conway Damer (1748-1828) daughter of his close friend the Hon. Henry Conway was an object of especial admiration. He left her the life tenancy of Strawberry Hill and an income to maintain it. Her work received a certain amount of respect amongst professionals and she was a frequent exhibitor at the Royal Academy. After Walpole's death she lived for a time at Strawberry Hill and then moved to York House in the centre of Twickenham.

The Waldegrave family later became owners of Strawberry Hill and the widow of the 7th Earl was famous as a hostess. A regular guest was Edward Lear (1812-1888) who as well as his famous coloured lithographs of parrots (sponsored by the Society of Arts) and his illustrated *Book of Nonsense*, exhibited landscapes at the Royal Academy and the British Institution.[1]

RIVER GODS AND ARTIST ARCHITECTS

In his play within a play *The Spanish Armada* by 'Mr Puff' which R.B.Sheridan (1751-1816), an insecure tenant of 'Lacy House' by the river at St Margarets, embodied in *The Critic* (1779), 'the Thames' appears personified. Other actors play the river's banks, one crowned with a model villa and another with osiers. In this way Sheridan invited his audiences to laugh at a long-standing English tradition which saw the Thames as a river god: Father Thames being the native equivalent of 'Father Tiber'. Verrio had painted such a figure for the Great Hall at Chelsea Hospital, Francis Hayman for the Rotunda at Vauxhall Gardens and James Barry for the Great Room of the Society of Arts in the Adelphi. By the 1780s it was possible to buy a nine foot long sculpture of *The River God Thames* moulded by the Society of Arts prodigy, John Bacon RA (1740-99) in Mrs Eleanor Coade's artificial stone. Derived from Bernini's celebrated fountain of the rivers in Rome, Bacon's deity emerges from a rocky base and pours waters from an enormous urn. At Ham House one was put up in the courtyard (c.1799) where it can still be seen, as can another in the Terrace Gardens on the Richmond bank. As well as this latter-day essay in the baroque, the Coade Company could cater for ecclesiastical gothic and neo-classical tastes. The lion cast for the Lambeth Brewery

---

[1] Simpson (1993), pp.26, 58; BOTLHS *Paper 69*, p.26; *ODNB* under Edward Lear.

to a design by William Woodington ARA (1806-93) survived the London Blitz and now stands at the south east end of Westminster Bridge. The same brewery originally had two more smaller Coade/Woodington lions. One was destroyed, but the other now stands at Twickenham stadium, where it represents the British and Irish Lions rugby football team.

In 1772 Horace Walpole ordered a Coade stone gateway for Strawberry Hill based on the tomb of a medieval bishop. He thought Mrs Coade was overcharging so the gateway remained unbuilt. The Brentford Gateway to Syon House designed by Robert Adam in 1773 had been ornamented in the Pompeian style using an inferior artificial stone. In 1814, to the order of the 2nd Duke of Northumberland, the work was restored using Coade stone; this has survived to the present day, as has the scagliola floor in the ante-room of the house, a replacement done in 1831-2 of the original Adam design.[1]

John Bacon (1740-99), *The Thames in Coade Stone*, (engraving published by J. Sewell, 1786)

The work of Robert Adam at Syon stemmed from the immense riches of Sir Hugh Smithson (1715-86). By his marriage to Lady Elizabeth Seymour Sir Hugh, already a man of great wealth, became heir to all the Percy properties including Syon House. His father-in-law, the so-called 'proud' Duke of Somerset, had used Syon as a summer residence and hunting lodge. He had continued the planting of tree-lined avenues noted by seventeenth century visitors. Sir Hugh admired the riverside view of the house and he employed Canaletto to paint one of his *Venice by the Thames* evocations: 'Mr Canaletti [sic] has begun the picture of Syon and by the outlines on canvas I think it will have a noble effect' he wrote in 1749. By the next year, 1750, as Earl and soon to be Duke of Northumberland he began to plan

James Tassie (1735-99), *Robert Adam* (portrait medallion, Jasperware)

the transformation of the property which he found 'ruinous and inconvenient' into 'a palace of Graeco-Roman splendour'. He employed Adam, the most

---

1   A. Kelly, *Mrs Coade's Stone* (London, 1990), pp.62, 371.

Canaletto (1697-1768), *Syon House*, 1749 (oil, Alnwick Castle. Collection of the Duke of Northumberland)

fashionable architect of the day and a fellow member of the Society of Arts, to create within the crenellated Tudor exterior a magnificent suite of rooms. This begins with a great hall where a clever arrangement of steps embellished with a screen of Doric columns disguises the uneven floor levels. Then follows the ante-room lavishly gilded, and with the scagliola floor already mentioned; the dining room with its richly ornamented apses screened by Corinthian columns at each end; the red drawing room with its crimson silk walls; and the long gallery, a glittering neo-classical interpretation of a seventeenth century form. Working for Adam and the Duke were Andrea Casali (1705-84), John Baptiste Cipriani RA (1727-85), William Marlow (1740-1813) and Francesco Zuccarelli RA (1702-89). Francis Lindo, a local Isleworth artist, painted portrait medallions of the Percy family (including imaginary likenesses of the Emperor Charlemagne and Harry Hotspur!) for the Long Gallery. The master mason Joseph Rose moulded the curved ceiling in the Red Drawing Room to resemble one in the Villa Madonna in Rome.[1]

Adam's work, which has survived almost intact at Syon, may also be found in varying states of preservation throughout the area. His transformation of Osterley Park on the fringes of the area remains in a pristine state, and Gordon House on the riverbank at St Margarets has the fine interior rooms he created in

[1] Richard Paulthorpe, et.al., *Syon Park* [Guide] (Derby, 2003), pp.39-55.

Eric Fraser (1902-82), *Garrick's Temple of Shakespeare and* [St Mary's] *Church at Hampton 1769*, (pen & ink and process white. Orleans House Gallery. Reproduced by permission of the Fraser family)

GARRICK'S *Temple of Shakespeare & Church at Hampton 1769*

1758 for General Humphrey Bland. The Green House 'executed to a classical design' for the General has long since been demolished though the design has been preserved. Inevitably, it might be said, there were commissions and disagreements over furniture and wall treatments with Horace Walpole at Strawberry Hill. David Garrick sought Adam's help with his buildings at Hampton and the villa, though damaged by fire in 2008, and the Temple to Shakespeare remain.

Garrick's links with the Adam Brothers are a reminder of the actor-author's patronage of the arts and his need to be abreast of taste. He was painted, as we have mentioned, as *Richard III* by Francis Hayman, and by Reynolds as *Between the Muses of Comedy and Tragedy*. He commissioned Roubiliac to produce his statue of Shakespeare and was an intimate friend of Hogarth. When sitting for Hogarth in 1757 he teased the great artist by making faces. The resulting work, which shows Garrick trying to write a prologue while Eve Maria (his wife) tries to steal his pen, is characteristically 'Hogarthian'. Johan Zoffany's portrayal of the couple on the lawn at Hampton reflect the influence of the master. Garrick's epitaph on

William Hogarth (1697-1764), *David Garrick and his Wife* (engraved by H. Boase from the oil painting, 1757)

Hogarth's monument in the churchyard of St Nicholas Church in Chiswick is a tribute derived from both affection and admiration.[1]

---

[1]   Simpson (1993), pp.74-5; C. Parry-Wingfield, 'David Garrick and "the art of living"', *Proceedings of the Hugenot Society* XXVIII (2), 2004, pp. 176-185; R. Paulson, *Hogarth*, vol.3 (Cambridge, 1993), pp.285-6, 434.

PART FOUR : 19TH CENTURY

The Genius of Landscape and the Photographic Interlude

TURNER

In the hagiography of artists from Vasari to Vertue and Walpole, as with the lives of inventors and industrialists memorialised by Samuel Smiles, early proficiency is a pre-requisite. Thus stories are told of Turner as an infant 'drawing with his finger in milk spilt on a tea tray' and how as a child in his parents' home in Covent Garden he would lie on the floor or sit at a table copying pictures, engravings and advertisements in newspapers or handbills. In 1785 at the age of ten he came to our area, being sent to stay with an uncle at Brentford, where he attended a local school and developed that passion for the historical topography of England and Europe and for classical mythology which, combined with a keen observation of riverside life-styles and scenery, would form the basis of so much of his art in the future.[1]

George Dance (1741-1825), *J.W.M. Turner, Esq. RA, PP,* (lithograph published by William Smith, 1827 after drawing dated 1800)

Turner's stay in Brentford may have lasted little more than a year and would be followed in 1789 by his admission to the Royal Academy Schools. In 1793 he was awarded 'The Greater Silver Palette' of the Society of Arts (see p.53). He was elected ARA in 1799 and become a full Academician in 1802. As a prosperous and acclaimed professional artist he could now afford to rise above the

[1]   A. Bailey, *Standing in the Sun: a life of J.M.W. Turner* (London, 1997), p.9.

J.M.W. Turner (1775-1851), *The Thames near Isleworth*, 1805 (pencil & watercolour, Tate Gallery)

humble circumstances of his early life. In 1805 he rented Syon Ferry House, on the banks of the Thames at Isleworth and either had built or purchased a river craft of his own which he would sail along the banks to Kew and Richmond and upstream to Teddington, Kingston and Hampton Court. Surviving Isleworth sketch books show how he would pull into the river bank to record a particular scene. Moving clouds, passing light, rainbows, shadowed or sunlit trees, fisher folk or passers-by, barges and wherries, were all recorded in these watercolours, charming to us today in their unfinished state, and valued by the artist as sources for completed lithographs and paintings.

When the lease of the house at Isleworth was due to expire Turner rented another one at Upper Mall, Hammersmith, also by the river. In 1807 he bought a plot of land at Twickenham in an area called Sandpit Close, which was a small eminence to the west of Cambridge Park and with views of Richmond Hill and Reynolds' former residence. Acting with great relish as his own architect and building contractor he built for himself an unostentatious villa with whitened stucco walls, sloping slate roofs and restrained neo-classical ornamentation. First known as 'Solus Lodge' it had been given its present name 'Sandycombe Lodge' by 1814. The garden was planted with willows, chestnuts and hawthorn. There was an oak tree out of which blackbirds flew. Inside the rooms were quite small except for the domed entrance hall which showed the influence of Turner's friend, Sir John Soane. In the dining room was a black marble fireplace surmounted by Francis Chantrey's *Paul at Iconium*. Chantrey (1781-1841) was a much admired sculptor, a Royal Academician and member of the Society of Arts who had married a wealthy Twickenham cousin. He and Turner often went fishing together using the boat the artist still kept at Isleworth.[1]

During his years at Twickenham, Turner was in regular touch with the Trimmer family at Heston. The Revd Henry Scott Trimmer, a keen amateur painter, was Vicar of Heston from 1804 until his death in 1859, and his son Henry Syer Trimmer had artistic ambitions. In return for coaching the son, Turner received lessons in Latin and Greek from the father. The three men would go on sketching expeditions together and report on their adventures to Mrs Trimmer. On one occasion they visited Osterley House to look at the painting collection and in the evening, greatly to Mrs Trimmer's interest, Turner drew from memory a sketch of a Gainsborough they had seen there as well as a sketch of a woman gathering watercress they had seen on the way.[2]

William Havell (1782-1857), *Sandycombe Lodge, Twickenham, Villa of J.M.W. Turner, RA* (engraved by W.B. Cooke 1829 after Havell's watercolour)

The water-colourist, William Havell (1782-1857) who had known Turner since their student days painted an often reproduced and engraved view entitled *Sandycombe Lodge, Twickenham, the Seat of J.M.W. Turner, RA* (1814). This

---

1   C. Parry-Wingfield, *A Brief Account of Sandycombe Lodge* (London, 2006), passim; Bailey (1997), pp.224-6; Simpson (1993), pp.36-7, 82-4; D. Hill, *Turner on the Thames* (New Haven and London, 1993), p.58; S. Moses, *Turner upon Thames* (Richmond, 2006), passim.

2   Bailey (1997), pp.229-30.

symbolised the barber's son's climb to social eminence in the neighbourhood which brought him to the notice of the Duke of Wellington, the Prince Regent and of Louis Philippe, Duke of Orleans and future King of the French.

Turner's ownership of Sandycombe Lodge and therefore his direct link with Twickenham came to an end in 1826 when he sold the property, though he long retained a house on the river downstream. He had, however planned to build a college or almshouses for impoverished English artists on land he owned near Twickenham Green. In 1829 following his father's death he made a will leaving the residue of his estate after small bequests and annuities to relatives and dependants and endowments at the Royal Academy and the Artists' Benevolent Institution, to the Twickenham College. This was now to be restricted to impoverished landscape painters and to have a gallery where the public could view their works. As is well known Turner's will was disputed after his death in 1851. In 1856 the Court of Chancery ruled in favour of the relatives, the Royal Academy and the named charities, but 'Turner's Gift' for the Twickenham College was held to be invalid.[1]

Sandycombe Lodge passed through various hands until 1947 when it came into the ownership of Professor Harold Livermore (1914-2010) who in conjunction with 'The Friends of Turner's House', established a trust early in the present century for its continued use as a centre for Turner studies. Professor Livermore, with the help of his late wife Ann, filled the house with a collection of Turner memorabilia. On his death in 2010 he made a bequest of this exceptional building to the nation as a monument to Turner.[2]

Three eminent artist friends of Turner who visited or passed through the area were John Varley (1778-1842), Edwin Landseer (1802-73) and Daniel Maclise (1811-70). Varley rented a house 'near Twickenham' in the summer of 1806 for himself and his pupils John Linnell (1792-1882) and William Henry Hunt (1790-1882). Landseer and Maclise were both guests of Dickens at Ailsa Park in 1838.[3] Another was W. P. Frith (1819-1909) who would paint many Dickensian subjects. Frith recalled in his *Memoirs* a sad, albeit amusing, trip to Hampton Court in 1842 to hear his teacher Henry Sass (1788-1844) lecture on the Raphael cartoon. Sass's dementia was developing and as the coach neared Hampton he persuaded the driver to demonstrate the working of a 'Gibus' by sitting on his (Sass's) until then rigid, top hat. The return journey was on Sass's insistence performed partly in and out of the river.[4]

Henry Pether (fl. 1828-1865) was the third generation of a family of landscape

---

1   Bailey (1997), pp.260, 402-4.
2   Parry-Wingfield (2006), pp.22-5; information supplied by Prof. Harold Livermore in 2009.
3   Simpson (1993), pp.36, 78.
4   N. Wallis, ed, *The Memoirs of W. P. Frith* (London, 1957), pp.35-6.

Henry Pether
(1828-1865),
*Twickenham by
Moonlight*, 1835
(oils, Richmond
Borough Art
Collection, Orleans
House Gallery)

painters, all of whom specifically and somewhat eccentrically specialised in moonlit scenes. Much as his series of Thames paintings, his *Twickenham by Moonlight*, 1835, touches closely upon the contemporary romanticism of Caspar David Friedrich. Eel Pie Island is counterbalanced by St Mary's church, but the Thames dominates under the play of moonlight.

THE HILDITCHES, THE DELAMOTTES AND OTHER SOCIETY OF ARTS PRIZE WINNERS

The two brothers George Hilditch (1803-1857) and Richard Henry Hilditch (d.1873) both became known for their watercolour sketches of local views. A contemporary enthusiast wrote of them in 1824: 'their productions evince superior genius, and aided by their well known passionate love of the art, their names bid fair to descend to posterity.' Their father was a wealthy city business man who liked to spend the summer months in Twickenham, where he engaged a local landscape painter, Thomas Christopher Hofland (1777-1843) to give advice and instruction to the boys. Hofland specialised in close imitations of Claude and Poussin, Wilson and Gainsborough. He was also a passionate angler and campaigned like Francis Francis (1822-86),

Anon, *George Hilditch* (1803-57) (1887 print from a photograph, Richmond Borough Art Collection, Orleans House Gallery)

George Hilditch (1803-57) LEFT: *View of Richmond Bridge*, 1844 (oil, Richmond Borough Art Collection, Orleans House Gallery) RIGHT: *King Street, Twickenham*, 1860 (photograph, Richmond Borough Art Collection, Orleans House Gallery)

a better known and later Twickenham fisherman, for the preservation of fish stocks. He taught the boys to combine fishing with sketching expeditions on the riverside. George and Henry both attended the Royal Academy Schools and would in later life recall amusing anecdotes of the great Turner.

George proved the more successful. Though he gave some of his time to the family business he competed for the Society of Arts awards, receiving a gold medal in 1823, a large silver medal in 1824 and a smaller silver medal in 1825. From 1823 to within a year of his death he was a regular exhibitor at the Royal Academy and the British Institution, a rival exhibiting body founded in 1805 under the influence of the Society of Arts. His work was at once dramatic and photographic in its detail and it comes as no surprise that he was an early experimenter with photography. In 1852 he contributed to the first exhibition of photography, which was held by the newly formed 'Photographic Society' under the auspices of the Society of Arts in the Adelphi. The titles of his exhibits, such as *Richmond Bridge* and *A Street in Twickenham* reflect his long term interest in the locality. Surviving prints made from his negatives by his nephew, J.B. Hilditch, c.1900, indicate that the originals were calotypes, which accounts for their peculiar clarity and timeless quality.[1]

[1] Richmond Athenaeum, *Catalogue* [for May Day conversazione] (Richmond, 1889) passim; Carolyn Blore, *From Canvas to Camera. George Hilditch 1803-57* (Richmond, 2000), passim; Information supplied by Dr Carolyn Blore, 2009.

Society of Arts
palette and medals

Exhibiting in company with George Hilditch at the Photographic Exhibition of 1852 were two other local artists: Philip Henry Delamotte (1821-89) of Belmont Place c.1850-67, 11 Clifden Road c.1867, then 'Grosvenor Lodge', Grosvenor Road, and Hugh Welch Diamond (1808-86) who lived at 'Twickenham House' from c.1858 onwards.

Philip Delamotte was the son of William Delamotte, Professor of Landscape Drawing at the Sandhurst Royal Military Academy, friend to both Girtin, who influenced his work, and Turner, who advised him on the planning of a sketching tour. Philip followed his father's career as a drawing master, being at one point employed by Queen Victoria to teach her grandchildren and holding for many years the Chair of Fine Art at King's College London. He published a large number of books on such varied subjects as printing, engraving, photography and sketching. His photographs of Strawberry Hill illustrate the ability he shared with George Hilditch to produce an image of satisfying and arranged realism.[1]

Philip Delamotte (1821-89), *Self portrait*, c.1852 (photograph, collection of A.J. Stirling)

[1] BOTLHS *Paper 69*, pp.13, 26; A.J. Stirling, 'Philip Henry Delamotte: artist and photographer', *Jnl.RSA* CXXXVIII (1990), pp.491-95.

Philip Delamotte (1821-89), *The Long Gallery, Strawberry Hill*, 1863 (photographs)

For Hugh Welch Diamond (1808-86), Doctor of Medicine, realism was all important. In 1858 he opened a private asylum for insane female patients at Twickenham House which he maintained down to his death in 1886. Described as 'the father of psychiatric photography', he systematically documented various forms of mental illness, with specific purpose; as a record of the appearance of patients with different psychiatric conditions; as a means of identification for readmission and categorisation; and to present to the patient as an accurate self-image as an aid to their treatment. Elizabeth Twining (1805-89) who lived in the family home of Dial House and also won Society of Arts' awards for her watercolours of flowers, is chiefly remembered as the tireless patron of St John's Hospital, which Diamond would have often visited.

Hugh Welch Diamond (1809-86), *An incumbent, Surrey County Lunatic Asylum*, c.1852 (photograph)

Hablot Knight Browne (1815-82), *Twickenham Ferry* (drawn and engraved as an illustration to C.Dickens, *Little Dorrit*, 1857)

Hablot Knight Browne (1815-82) was a youthful prize winner of the Society of Arts, gaining silver medals in 1832 and 1833. Like so many of his contemporaries he was adept at topographical scenes and was familiar with the Twickenham area. Under the alias of 'Phiz' he became famous as the illustrator of Dickens' works, including the view of Twickenham Ferry he produced for *Little Dorrit* which perfectly captured the atmosphere described by the novelist:

Thomas Rowlandson (1757-1827), *Eel Pie Island*, c.1809 (engraved from an ink and watercolour drawing)

Within view was the peaceful river and the ferry-boat…thus runs the current always. Let the heart swell into what discord it will, thus plays the rippling water in the prow of the ferry-boat ever the same tune. Year after year, so much allowance for the drifting of the boat, so many miles an hour the flowing of the stream, here the rushes, there the lilies, nothing uncertain or unquiet.[1]

The excursion to Eel Pie Island described by Dickens in *Nicholas Nickleby* was unfortunately not illustrated. This rumbustious haven for early 19th century day trippers is given graphic form by Thomas Rowlandson (1757-1827) in a view showing merrymakers disembarking on the island. Rowlandson seems himself to have made a trip from London to the area in 1809 since he also drew views of Richmond riverside, Ham House and Strawberry Hill. Later in the century the dubious pleasures of boat travel were recorded by Alfred Cooper in his 1862 print *All Adrift: a Scene on the Thames at Twickenham.*[2]

---

[1]   Charles Dickens, *Little Dorrit*, (London, 1857), p.146; Simpson (1993), p.78; D.G.C. Allan, *'Barkiss is willin'*, *some Dickensian associations of the Society of Arts*, WSG *Occasional Paper* 5 (London, 2009), passim.

[2]   Simpson (1993), pp.36, 79, 125; B. Gascoigne and J. Ditchburn, *Images of Twickenham* (Richmond, 1981), Catalogue no.314, p.314.

Alfred W. Cooper (fl.1863-1903), *All Adrift: a Scene on the Thames at Twickenham*, 1862 (print from watercolour published April 1862)

JAMES GOOCH'S VIEWS
AND THE ORLEANS HOUSE CIRCLE

Whereas George Hilditch's photographs record Twickenham of the 1850s and 1860s, the period when street lanterns made their appearance in front of the *George Inn*, James Gooch's fine lithographs of 1832, like 'Phiz's' peaceful scene, give a picture of the little town first emerging from its rural past. A former inhabitant of Norfolk where he was said to have been a pupil of Crome, Gooch would have felt at home amongst the pantiled roofs and weatherboarding he depicts, together with hay carts of various sizes, mounted fruit vendors with panniers, cattle driven down the middle of King Street, the town beadle looking with some suspicion across the road at a boy trundling a wheelbarrow in front of the *George*. A view from the Surrey bank showing Twickenham Ait, later renamed Eel Pie Island, probably shows a 'swan-upping' ceremony at which Gooch would have played some official role. Appointed Vestry Clerk of St Mary's in 1833, other public offices held by this artistic administrator included Registrar of Births and Deaths and Census Registrar from 1841 to 1861, Collector of Rates, Assistant Overseer of the Poor, and Clerk to the Highways Board. He was Clerk to the Tithes Commission in 1845.[1]

Gooch's lithographs are ante-dated by an unsigned view of 1817, which is interesting because it shows the Georgian mansion known as 'Highshot House' at the end of Crown Road, with the princely occupant of a carriage being respectfully saluted by a file of neatly clad children and their fashionably dressed charges.

---

[1]   Simpson (1993), p.85.

James Gooch
(c.1784-1872),
*Eel Pie Island
Twickenham,*
1832 (lithograph,
Richmond
Borough Art
Collection, Orleans
House Gallery)

James Gooch (c.1784-1872),
King Street, Twickenham, 1832
(lithograph, Richmond Borough Art
Collection, Orleans House Gallery)

James Gooch (c.1784-1872),
*London Road, Twickenham, looking
south*, 1832 (lithograph, Richmond
Borough Art Collection, Orleans
House Gallery)

Unknown artist,
Highshot House, 1817
(lithograph)

Edouard Pingret (1788-1875), *Visit of Louis Philippe, King of the French, to Orleans House, 1844*
(lithograph by Pingret, 1846, Richmond Borough Art Collection, Orleans House Gallery)

In 1800 Louis Philippe, Duke of Orleans, and his two younger brothers came as
hard-up exiles to live in Highshot. His brothers died after a few years and Louis
left for France in 1814, returning a year later again as an exile but now possessed
of great wealth. He moved to Secretary Johnston's House, today called 'Orleans
House', living there until 1817 when the lithograph was drawn. Another French
nobleman, the Comte de Jarnac, who lived at nearby Sion Row, did a watercolour sketch of Orleans House. The Duke's ADC, General Laurent Athalin,
who lived at Ferry House, was another amateur artist who spent time sketching
Twickenham views, which have survived as prints. The July Revolution of 1830
in France swept Louis Philippe to the throne. During his 1844 state visit, as guest
of Queen Victoria, the King came from Windsor to revisit his old home, an occasion recorded by visiting French artist Edouard Pingret in a much reproduced
lithograph *The visit of Louis Philippe, King of the French to Orleans House, 1844*.[1]

In 1864 the King's grandson, Louis Philippe Albert, Comte de Paris, returned
to Twickenham to live at York House. He sold the property in 1876 to an Indian

---

[1]   BOTLHS *Paper 49*, p.7; Simpson (1993), pp.39, 93.

Administrator and Society of Arts lecturer, Sir Mountstuart Elphinstone Grant Duff, remembered in Twickenham as a friend of celebrities and royal personages. 'Tiny' Grant Duff, Sir Mountstuart's daughter, made friends of the rather hardup, albeit well connected Peel sisters who lived with their parents in the area. Carli Peel, who had studied art in Bristol, commuted by train from Twickenham to Vauxhall where she improved her technique at a studio run by a Mr Furze. She soon found she could supplement her income by selling drawings for publication in *The Queen* magazine. Charlotte Peel earned her money as a journalist, but none of these commercial actions were considered a bar to their mixing with the Duchess of Teck and Princess Mary at York House, which again became the home of the Orleans Prince and Princess in the late 1890s. In the meantime Orleans House itself had been bought by the Cunard family who lent it for the wedding breakfast of Princess Hélène in 1895.[1]

Ethel Chapman Nisbet of Heath Road, like Charlotte Peel, was an upper middle class lady. A regular exhibitor at the Royal Academy and at the Women's Watercolour Society, she specialised in watercolours, painted still lifes and fine architectural studies; her particular talent for flower painting led her to publish reproductions of her works in instructional book form. Ethel's name has been linked with that of Laura Cunard, another lady amateur. She was the daughter-in-law of Lady Susan Cunard, who was herself active in The New English Art Club. The 'New English' Group had begun as a progressive academic movement similar to the French Impressionists. Turner, whom the Impressionists admired, had shown how our river could inspire experiments with light and colour.[2]

Ethel Nisbet, (exh.1882-1916), Flower Painting for Beginners (Blackie & Son, 1890); and Daisies; Pansy (watercolour ilustrations)

1   Simpson (1993), p.94; BOTLHS *Paper 69*, p.27; C.S. Peel, *Life's Enchanted Cup: an autobiography 1872-1933* (London, 1933), pp.61-3.

2   Ethel Nisbet, *Flower Painting for Beginners* (London, 1890); BOTLHS *Paper 24*; Simpson (1993), p.23; J. Hone, *The Life of Henry Tonks* (London, 1939), pp.94-7.

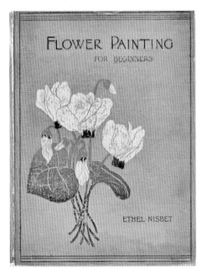

ABOVE: Alfred Sisley (1839-99), *Bridge at Hampton Court*, 1874 (oils, Wallraf-Richartz Museum, Cologne, © Rheinisches Bildarchiv Köln)

RUGHT: Paula Nightingale (1937-), *Interpretations of a Sisley riverscape*, 2008 (oils, artist's collection)

In 1874 Alfred Sisley journeyed up the Thames to Hampton where he used his technique of divided colour and spontaneous brush strokes with blue and violet shadows and orange-gold and tawny pigment. In the 21st century Paula Nightingale teaches her students on the sites used by Sisley for his Hampton paintings.[1]

<hr />

[1]   J. Sheaf and K. Howe, *Hampton and Teddington Past* (London, 1995), p.44; Paula Nightingale 'In the Footsteps of Alfred Sisley', *Artists and Illustrators*, issue 272 (April 2009), pp.71-3.

PART FIVE : EARLIER 20TH CENTURY

Expressionists, Collectors and Amateurs

WARTIME SHADOWS

The stone crosses in the churchyard of St Mary's, Twickenham and of Holy Trinity, Twickenham Green, and Mortimer Brown's bronze soldier with rifle and pack in Radnor Gardens were sad reminders for the people of Twickenham of the losses suffered by so many families in the Great War of 1914-18, and other monuments were to be found at Isleworth, Teddington and Hampton. Brian Pearce has written of Virginia Woolf's sensitivity to the aftermath of this great conflict and of her friend, the artist Duncan Grant's links with Lytton Strachey, a pacifist by conviction.[1] The landscape of the river bank from Richmond to Twickenham and of Bushy Park and Hampton Court could be a solace for writers and painters. Tea and sympathy could be found at Lucy Millet's Studio at Hampton Wick and at the shows of the Thames Valley Arts Club which she

Mortimer Brown (1874-1966), *Statue of Soldier* [Twickenham War Memorial] (bronze, signed 1921, erected 1926, Radnor Gardens, Twickenham.
Photograph: Ronald Sim)

had founded. An exhibitor at the 1932 Thames Valley exhibition bore the ominous title of the 2nd Earl of Ypres, being the son of the Field Marshal Sir John French, 1st Earl of Ypres whose name and title conjure up images of the carnage

---

[1] Simpson (1993), pp.133-7; BOTLHS *Paper 87*, pp.16, 30; M Chamet, D. Farrand and Martin Butler, *The Modern British Paintings, Drawings and Sculpture* (London, 1964) under Mortimer Brown (1874-1966).

of the trenches. A resident of Ivy House, Hampton Court, Lord Ypres was an accomplished amateur whose landscape watercolours were praised for their 'delicate and transparent colour'. The Thames Valley artists struggled on during the second great conflict (1939-45) which would see Lilian Dring transforming rags into artistic riches, Eric Fraser cheering the home front with his *Radio Times* vignettes, while air raids damaged Syon and destroyed Radnor House and accidental fires gutted Isleworth Church and Buxted Park.[1] The deep air raid shelters built at the back of Twickenham College await exploration.

DUNCAN GRANT AND MARGARET GEDDES

Duncan Grant was born in 1885 when his parents were home on leave from India. In 1894 he was sent to live with his aunt Lady Grant at Hogarth House, Chiswick. After attending the Westminster School of Art and the Slade he was introduced by his cousin Lytton Strachey to Roger Fry and Vanessa Bell who founded the Omega Workshops in 1913. Grant was both an innovative textile and pottery designer and a landscape painter of genius. In 1919 after years spent in India, Grant's parents settled at Grosvenor House, Grosvenor Road, Twickenham, the former home of P. H. Delamotte, where they were frequently visited by their son. It was during these visits that Duncan drew his

Duncan Grant (1885-1978), *Portrait photograph*, 1920

River View, Twickenham c.1928, a sketch showing Richmond Hill rising above the river and painted his *Twickenham Scene* c.1930, a view of the cottages near the *Barmy Arms* pub, and his *Twickenham in the Snow* 1940, a view of St Mary's Church seen above the houses and trees on the Twickenham Embankment. Grant recorded an occasion in July 1928 which has a decidedly 'Turneresque' ring: 'This morning was grey but rather lovely. I took a punt and began to sketch from the river – but the tide kept swinging me round and round and the steamers kept me rocking – so I had a very difficult time.'[2]

Like his other 'Bloomsbury Group' friends Grant saw the arts in the context of intellectual endeavour. Osbert Sitwell recalled how he would enunciate his theories of art in lengthy harangues when he became oblivious of his physical

---

[1]   See following sections, and Part Six

[2]   BOTLHS *Paper 87*, pp.30-37; A. Bertram, *A Century of British Painters 1851-1951* (London, 1951) plate 51.

Duncan Grant (1885-1978),
Twickenham Scene, c.1930 (oils,
private collection)

surroundings. Sitwell was once listening to the artist and saw him fall down to
the bottom of a long steep flight of stairs, holding in one hand a candlestick with
a lighted candle in it, and 'apparently without having noticed his tumble, and
certainly without having allowed his candle to go out, continued his talk where
he had left it off as soon as he regained the landing.'[1]

[1]   O. Sitwell, *Noble Essences*, (London, 1950), p.167. Sitwell said the episode occurred 'some
      quarter of a century ago' which would make it roughly contemporary with Grant's equally
      absent-minded handling of the punt at Twickenham.

Duncan Grant
(1885-1978),
*Twickenham in
the Snow*, 1940
(oils, 38 x 48 cm,
private collection)

Margaret Geddes (1914-98) was nineteen years younger than Duncan Grant but no doubt would have learnt of his work when she too studied at the Westminster School of Art. Amongst her teachers was Grant's friend Max Gertler. At the Westminster Margaret began her long pilgrimage from an English impressionist realism to experimental use of abstract form. After the second world war which saw the closure of the Westminster, following Gertler's tragic suicide, Margaret came to live and work in Teddington. Although her national and international reputation grew, she tended to hide her artistic fame from her local friends and associates. By the

Margaret Geddes (1914-98) in her Teddington studio, 1964.
Photograph: John Foster-Turner

1960s she had achieved fame as a President of the Women's International Art Club and as a regular exhibitor at the Redfern Gallery. In 1966 she summarised her technique:

> My method is to approach the canvas with nothing between myself and it – so that I am forced into a dialogue with it...taking the plunge without conscious direction [and] following up hints given by the painting, allowing images to form themselves before knowing what they are.

She continued to live and work in Teddington for the next thirty years although the onset of Alzheimer's disease in the 1980s restricted her output. She died in 1998 at a nursing home in Taunton to which she had been moved in the previous year. As her biographer put it:

> Her world was an intensely private and personal one, and her paintings were emotionally exhausting to produce. She had absolutely no thoughts of 'career', notions of self-advancement, or any beliefs other than that painting was a demanding and painfully serious business which could not be compromised.[1]

THE IONIDES FAMILY

In 1927 The Hon Mrs Nellie Levy (1883-1962), the widow of Walter Levy (d.1923) and daughter of the 1st Viscount Bearsted, purchased the surviving portions of Orleans House, including the historically and architecturally significant 'Octagon' with an adjacent wing and stable block. With the assistance of her second husband, the architect and interior designer, Basil Ionides FRIBA FRSA (1884-1950), she built up an extensive collection of works of art, many of

---

[1]   D.J. Wilcox, *Margaret Geddes* (London, 1998) , passim and pp. 35, 55-7.

Tea break at the Hampton Wick School of Art.
This photograph taken by her great-nephew shows
Mrs Millet presiding in her studio, 1935.

Lucy Millet (fl.c.1880-1948), *View from the Old Castle
Wharf Studio, Hampton Wick*, [n.d.] (line drawing, TVAC)

which relate to the Twickenham and Richmond areas. In 1931 a year after their
marriage Mr & Mrs Ionides bought Buxted Park and restored the house and
grounds. She also purchased the Jacobean Manor House, Whitton Dean, where
she would be often visited by Queen Mary, who encouraged her collecting enthu-
siasms. She reluctantly gave up the Manor House when it became surrounded
by new estates, but salvaged the gate posts which still stand in the grounds of
Buxted Park. In 1940 Buxted Park House was largely destroyed by fire and although Basil endeavoured to rebuild it in the immediate post-war years, the main
family home became 'Riverside House' adjacent to Orleans House. In 1956 Mrs
Ionides announced her intention of bequeathing her riverside properties and her
collection of paintings to the local authority, and after her death in 1962 steps
were taken to establish the present day Orleans Gallery.[1]

THE THAMES VALLEY ARTS CLUB AND OTHER LOCAL 'REALISTS'

Lucy Constance Marian Millet (1880-1948) studied at the Lambeth School of
Art, at South Kensington and the Royal Academy Schools, and in France and
Belgium. In the 1890s she settled with her sister firstly at 11 Seymour Road,
Hampton Wick, and then at Gomer House on Lower Teddington Road; and her
studios were in Old Bridge Street and at the Malt House on Old Castle Wharf
adjacent to Gomer House. She seems in her early years to have commuted by
train to Vauxhall, where she taught at the Lambeth School, the first woman to
do so. Her own 'Hampton Wick School of Art' of which she was the Director,
and which she advertised as 'a continental studio by the Thames', became a

---

[1]   Information supplied by Mr Ed Harris; Simpson (1993), pp.29, 140; *Jnl.RSA*, 6 Oct., 1950.
      For eight months after the outbreak of War in September 1939 the RSA Office Staff were
      evacuated to Buxted Park.

flourishing local institution and a centre for professional and amateur artists. Lucy Millet created a pleasant and what was remembered as 'rather Bohemian' atmosphere in her school, where everyone wore artist's smocks and there would be tea intervals amidst the clutter of *bric à brac* and assorted paintings at which the model, the pupils and the distinguished patrons of the Thames Valley Arts Club would join the Director at table. Enoch Ward (1859-1922) was a prominent local professional whose studio in Old Castle Wharf encouraged Lucy in forming the network of talent which ensured the success of her school and club. Though her School did not survive her death the Club has continued with its regular exhibitions to the present day and treasures the memory of its foundress. The *Surrey Comet* for 15 September 1906 contained an enthusiastic review headed:

THAMES VALLEY ARTS CLUB
FIRST PUBLIC EXHIBITION OF MEMBERS' WORK

The reporter noted Lucy Millet as 'the most prolific exhibitor' having twenty-three pictures on view ranging from views of old cottages at Hampton Wick to scenes in Brittany. She earned praise for her 'eye for the picturesque and her ability to transfer it to canvas'. Hugo Tabor of Teddington was praised for his landscapes and his wife Hélène Tabor for her portraits. A certain Edith Gavey of Hampton exhibited *A misty morning, Richmond* and several flower pieces, but most of the hundred works on show have not been identified and we can only guess that original views of T.R. Way's lithographs of *Church Street* and *King Street, Twickenham* (1900) and E.B. Phipson's *Old Cottages in Bell Lane, Twickenham* (1904) were amongst them. The permission given by the Kingston Corporation to allow the use of the Municipal Art Gallery for the exhibition was gratefully recorded.

Many well-known figures in the art world would be associated with the TVAC over the years. Philip Connard RA (1876-1958) was a member; and exhibited three paintings as early as 1908. He became President in 1934 and remained so until 1949, in spite of becoming Keeper of the Royal Academy from 1945-49. He lived at Cholmondeley Lodge, by the river at Richmond, and was remembered for painting in the English impressionist tradition of restrained, atmospheric landscape art.

In May 1932 the Club celebrated its 50th Exhibition. It was a big show – over-crowded, according to one *Comet* reporter – consisting of 161 paintings and eight pieces of sculpture. William Shackleton (d.1933), then President, was, like Connard, a well-known figure, landscape and portrait painter. He exhibited two landscapes and a portrait at the Thames Valley show and had twelve works on show at the Royal Academy, that year.

John Fulwood (1854-1981), also an RA Exhibitor, a native of Birmingham, published exquisite dry-point etchings of the river at Hampton and Teddington. His

John Fulwood (1854-1931). LEFT: *Teddington Reach*, c.1920 RIGHT: *Hampton river view*, c.1920 (dry point etchings, private collection)

connections with the TVAC remain uncertain, though he is known to have had a house in Twickenham as well as a Birmingham home. A TVAC member at that time was Robert Catterson-Smith, the figure and landscape painter, whose works are in many permanent collections including the Walker Art Gallery, Liverpool, and the Manchester City Art Gallery, and who had often exhibited with the Royal Academy and the Royal Hibernian Academy. His portrait of his eldest son was said to be the focal point of the 50th Thames Valley Exhibition. Miss Isobel Catterson-Smith, his daughter, also a member, showed some flower paintings.

Although the Thames Valley Club never lost its identity as an association during the Second World War, only five exhibitions were held between 1939 and 1949. In 1949 it still had 73 members and there were 130 works on show at its exhibition. Of especial note were the paintings displayed by Terence Cuneo (1907-96). Son of Cyrus Cuneo, an established illustrator, Cuneo trained at Chelsea and the Slade, was a member of the War Artists Advisory Committee during the 2nd World War, and then travelled all over the world undertaking commissions which included an official painting of the Coronation of the Queen in Westminster Abbey. He became President of the TVAC in 1955. Under his Presidency and the Chairmanship of John Kingsley Sutton FRSA (d.1976) the Club gained in both strength and membership. In 1980 it published an official history and was still flourishing in 2006 when it celebrated its centenary. Today its meetings tend to be outside our area, either in Richmond, Kingston or Thames Ditton.[1]

While Hampton Wick saw this flowering of talent on its riverside, further downstream at Isleworth, Adrian Bury FRSA (1891-1991) maintained the tradition of the Thameside artists. Bury was the son of a far from wealthy sculptor and

[1] BOTLHS *Paper 69*, p.24, note 27; M. Rees, *The History of the Thames Valley Arts Club* (Surbiton, 1980), passim. Information on the TVAC supplied by Mrs Ann Ryves, Mr Michael Hart and Mr Peter Sandeman. Information on John Fulwood supplied by Miss Jane Baxter, LBRUT Reference Librarian, Local Studies Collection and Mr Ronald Sim. For T.R. Way's and E.D. Phipson's view of Twickenham (1904) see Simpson (1993), p.90, 127, 128.

Adrian Bury
(1891-1991), *The London Apprentice, 1937* (watercolour, 26.5 x 37cm, London Borough of Hounslow Local Studies Collection)

was forced at an early age to take journalistic work. Using money he had saved from his own wages he went to Paris to study at the Académie Julian. The start of the First World War interrupted his studies and he returned to England to join the army but was rejected on medical grounds. After several secretarial jobs he became literary editor of the *Sunday Pictorial* where he remained until 1922, when he made a lengthy tour of Italy to pursue his interest in art. On his return he commenced writing books on artists past and present as well as painting watercolours, which he regularly exhibited at the Royal Watercolour Society. In the 1930s and 1940s he lived in Church Street, Isleworth, and painted numerous local views.

Adrian Bury's obituary called him 'a fine landscape artist in the traditional English School who looked for inspiration from the past masters, especially Cotman, Peter de Wint and John Varley.' It noted his association with contemporaries such as Sir Alfred Munnings, Dame Laura Knight and Sir William Russell Flint. Bury shared with Russell Flint, who was an especially close friend, a love of the effect of absorbent watercolours. Official recognition came when he was created 'Laureate' of the Old Watercolour Society and awarded a civil list pension 'for services to British Art'.[1]

[1]   A. Bury, *Just a Moment, Time* (London, 1967), passim; *The Times*, 17 May 1991.

Jill Storey (1950-),
*Daffodils in
Marble Hill Park*
(watercolour,
artist's collection)

Jill Storey (1950-) whose home and studio is in Copthall Gardens, a turning off Heath Road near the historic heart of Twickenham, is a present day artist who paints very much in the style of Adrian Bury. She trained at Gloucestershire College of Art and then studied for the Post-graduate art teachers' certificate at Goldsmiths' College in London. She moved to Twickenham in 1980 and after ten years of teaching in various schools and colleges began painting and exhibiting professionally in 1990. Her work is mainly in watercolour and pastel and has been frequently reproduced in colour for use on greetings cards. Like Bury she has contributed to the exhibition of the Royal Institution of Painters in Watercolour and the Royal Watercolour Society. She has received commissions from the BBC, English Heritage, Kingston Grammar School, Richmond Environmental Trust and the Museum of Rugby at Twickenham.

Jill Storey's own words tell of her attachment to this area: 'I have always drawn great inspiration from the riverside at Twickenham – its changing moods and colours at different times of the day and through the seasons.'[1] A member of the Fountain Gallery, a co-operative of local artists based near Hampton Court, she is a regular exhibitor locally and at London venues.

The Teddington Group was founded in 1990 to include both professional and amateur artists and designers. Its number is limited to twelve – enough to fill an average size living room. Members are required to be Teddington residents and this geographical limit even excludes Strawberry Hill. Like the TVAC it

---

[1]   Communication from Mrs Jill Storey to the author, October 2009.

is an essentially exhibiting society, though the members show their work individually throughout the country. Annual Autumn exhibitions have been held at the Victorian Theatre in Normansfield and Bushy House. Midsummer 'Art Fairs', were begun in 1994 and are held at the Landmark Arts Centre which is in the deconsecrated church of St Alban at Teddington Lock. Though organised by the Group, the Fairs contain work by artists coming to Teddington from all over the country. Visitor numbers have averaged at least 3,000 and exhibitors generally total 80 or more.[1]   The sculptress Avril Vellacott (1941-) played a leading role in establishing the Teddington Artists: influenced at an early age by her grandfather E.W. Barnes (1880-1960), who was a successful commercial artist and amateur painter of portraits and landscapes and a TVAC exhibitor, Avril developed her skills through study at Kingston College of Art, at Dartington Hall and at the City and Guilds School

Avril Vellacott (1941-), *Noel Coward* (bronze, 1999), 'presented to the people of Teddington by the Teddington Society'.
Courtesy of Teddington Library.
Photograph: Peter Moore

of Art, Kennington, where she was awarded the Sculpture Prize on her graduation in 1982. She taught figurative and portrait sculpture at the Richmond Adult Community College from 1985-2005 and her busts of Dr John Langdon Haydon Down (1828-96), founder of Normansfield, of Noel Coward (1899-1973), youthful inhabitant of Waldegrave Road, and of the former Liberal Party Leader Jeremy Thorpe (1929-) – a House of Commons commission – all attracted great acclaim.[2]

[1]   Teddington Society Newsletter *Tidings* 2009, pp.6-7.

[2]   Information supplied by Avril Vellacott, 2010.

PART SIX : LATE 20TH AND INTO THE 21ST CENTURY

Applied Art, Art Education and Abstract Art

BRUSH, BLOCK AND NEEDLE

Four local artists are linked through their interest in applied art and education. Eric Fraser (1902-82), an illustrator and commercial artist of great skill and imagination, lived and worked at Penn's Place, Hampton. During World War II he worked on camouflage, subsequently returning to journalism and advertising. He had been educated at Westminster City School and had studied art at Goldsmiths' College. He taught at Camberwell College of Art, 1928-40, having begun drawing for *Radio Times* in 1926. Over the years he contributed work to *Harper's Bazaar*, *Vogue*, *The Listener*, *Art and Industry*, *The Studio* and *Lilliput Magazine* and to books published

Eric Fraser (1902-82), *To Die a King*, 1968 (pen & ink vignette for *Radio Times*. Ill. David Driver, *The Art of Radio Times*, 1981, p.146, reproduced by permission of the Fraser family)

by the Folio Society and the Golden Cockerel Press. He had works shown at the Royal Academy exhibitions and the Brussels International Exhibition (1958). The vignettes he drew for *Radio Times*, especially for the plays and features on the Third Programme, possessed an extraordinary quality of immediacy and dramatic force, rapidly establishing his name and style in the national artistic subconscious, while his charmingly whimsical 'Mr Therm' proved a recognisable symbol for British Gas for thirty years, appearing in a variety of topical, humoristic and instructive guises, as well as on gas products such as refrigerators. Gifted with an almost puritanical work ethic, Fraser was equally prolific in his support

FACING PAGE: St Mary the Virgin, Hampton.

LEFT: Eric Fraser (1902-82) *Gabriel, Uriel, Michael, Raphael*. Stained glass window, 1963. Raphael appears to have been fishing in the Thames, which provides the background, and features St Mary's Church and Garrick's temple.

RIGHT: Geoffrey Fraser (1927-), *The History of Hampton*. Mural, 1952-3.

By kind permission of the Vicar.
Photographs: Peter Moore

THIS PAGE:
RIGHT: Eric Fraser, *Self portrait*, 1949 (ink & charcoal)
FAR RIGHT: Geoffrey Fraser, *Self portrait*, 1952 (from the mural)

for the local community, providing graphics for the Twickenham Choral and other local societies. A committed Christian, he designed stained glass windows and altar fittings for St Mary the Virgin, Hampton, where he is himself commemorated in etched glass panels. In the same church the west wall is occupied by a mural featuring the local scene by his son, Rev. Geoffrey Fraser.[1]

Lilian Dring (1908-98) practised as a poster artist and was among the talented group commissioned by London Transport in the 1930s. During the war she settled in Teddington and in 1950 designed the superb piece, *The Patchwork of the Century*, for the Festival of Britain, first exhibited at York House, Twickenham, and then on the South Bank in 1951. A hundred patchwork squares chart a historic event for each year of the century 1851-1950. Eighty housewives with no previous experience or training in needlework completed this community project in just over two months. The theme and design of many of the panels were inspired by Lilian, but she encouraged other participants to create their own designs. Lilian herself completed the panels for '1851', '1871', '1921' and '1950'. Some of the

Lilian Dring (1908-98), *Underground Women*, 1986 (mixed media, London Transport Museum)

panels reflected the personal interests of the maker. Dorothy Marshall, a veteran woman scientist living in a Twickenham home who had studied at Girton College, Cambridge in the 1880s, provided the '1869' panel: the first of Lilian's volunteers, she insisted that her panel should depict Girton and this was drawn out ready for her to work. Her requirements met, Dorothy sewed the square, but later complained that the design showed too many windows. The '1855' panel, 'Florence Nightingale', was sewn at the instigation of the district nurse by

[1]   D. Driver, *The Art of Radio Times* (London, 1981); *Brush, block and needle* under Eric Fraser; Orleans House Gallery, *Eric Fraser (1902-82)* (posthumous exhibition, Twickenham, 1982).

The Patchwork of the Century, 1950 (embroidered patchwork, detail, 3m x 3m, Festival Hall, London. Courtesy of South Bank Centre Archive)

one of her patients. Old tablecloths, air force uniforms and blackout fabrics left over from the war were used in the patchwork. It is a credit to the patience and care of Lilian Dring that very little repair work has been necessary to maintain this motley collection of fabrics during the years in which it has been kept at the Royal Festival Hall.[1]

Osmund Caine (1914-2004) studied at Birmingham School of Arts and Crafts, returning after war service to teach life drawing. In 1948 he came south to live in Kingston, teaching at the Kingston School of Art and at the Twickenham College of Technology. In 1958 he instigated and headed the graphic design department at this latter, setting up broad-based vocational courses. Dedicated to the teaching of traditional art college skills such as life drawing, he combined these with innovative practice in book illustration, exhibition management and photography: while outside college he continued to produce designs for church windows in stained glass, an interest which had been kindled in his Birmingham years, reflecting his deeply held, though never paraded, Roman Catholic faith. Stanley Spencer was a major influence, seen, for example, in Caine's evocative *Wedding at Twickenham*, where, in the foreground, a tombstone bears his own name and that of his wife, Mary. His *Jam making in Twickenham* is in a happier, domestic mood. Significant as a statement on war and race, and akin to John

---

1   File marked 'Lilian Dring' in LBRUT, Reference Library, Local Studies Collection. Reference supplied by Miss Jane Baxter.

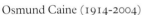

Osmund Caine (1914-2004)

ABOVE: Poster of Osmund Caine retrospective exhibition, featuring his *Jam making in Twickenham* (45x30cm, Orleans House Gallery, 1998)

UPPER RIGHT: *Wedding at Twickenham*, c.1960 (oil, Borough of Richmond Art Collection, Orleans House Gallery)

LOWER RIGHT: *Riverside at Kingston opposite Hampton Wick*, 1951 (oils, 37x53 cm, private collection)

Piper's tunnelled sleepers, was *Spider Hutments*, a painting Caine developed from a pencil sketch made during his wartime army days in Aldershot. Showing black and white squaddies in their barracks, it was only finished in 1985. Ten years before, in 1975, he had retired from the College but he continued to live in the large detached house on Kingston Hill, which he had bought in 1948. This he shared with his wife Mary, also an artist, and was where he brought up his family in bohemian disregard for modern comforts. He was sometimes a fiery figure, with as one of his sons said, 'a bellow that could fell an ox at a hundred yards'. College students stood in dread of his 'dressings down', though these could often be followed by carefully chosen avuncular advice leading to lasting friendships. Some like the designer Arthur Robins (1944-) expressed their gratitude to Caine 'for giving a no hoper a chance', many years after they had left the College.[1]

---

[1] Orleans House Gallery, *Osmund Caine (1914-2004)* exhibition catalogue (Twickenham, 2004); Obituary in *The Guardian* 2004. Information from Mr Arthur Robins, 2009.

Younger than Fraser, Dring and Caine, Felix Gluck (1923-81), passed his early life under the shadow of totalitarian regimes. Born in Bavaria into a family with Social Democratic sympathies he fled from the Nazis with his parents to Czechoslovakia in 1936 and from there to Hungary, studying at the Budapest Free Academy from 1941-44. Imprisoned in Mauthausen concentration camp 1944-45 he contracted tuberculosis, and subsequently spent two years recovering in a Davos, Switzerland, sanatorium. He came to England in 1948, and continued his studies at Durham,but was enticed back to Budapest in 1950, working as an illustrator for the Communist authorities who were becoming increasingly liberal in their policies. The Red Army crackdown on the 1956 rising made him once again a refugee,

Felix Gluck (1923-1981), *Self portrait*, 1943 (linocut, Borough of Richmond Local Studies Library)

taken in by friends in Richmond. Settling in Northcote Road, St Margarets, in 1962 he began a successful career as a graphic designer, teaching at Hornsey and Chelsea colleges, latterly 1973-77 at Twickenham College, and as an editor-publisher. He specialised in black and white wood- and lino-cuts, but was also an accomplished painter with an experimental bent. In 1970 he was elected a Member of the Society of Industrial Artists and a Fellow of the Royal Society of Arts. A posthumous exhibition of his work was mounted in 1981 at the Orleans House Gallery soon after his death.[1]

RICHMOND-UPON-THAMES COLLEGE AND THE RSA

Richmond-upon-Thames College was established in 1937 by Middlesex County Education Committee as 'Twickenham Technical Institute', and subsequently called the 'Twickenham College of Technology and School of Art'. It incorporated an 'Art Department' which had its origins in the Chiswick School of Art.

The characteristically 'art-deco' building designed by W.T. Curtis FRIBA and H.W. Burdett ARIBA consisted of a three storey façade faced with brown bricks laid in Dutch bond and flanked by two towers, that on the south end being above a dramatically enhanced entrance. Beyond the shorter north tower was

[1]   Orleans House Gallery, *Felix Gluck (1923-1981)*. Posthumous exhibition (Twickenham, 1981).

an arched entrance leading to a workshop quadrangle which in 1967 was linked to a 'Printing and Graphic Design Block'. The site chosen for the College was that of the former Marsh Farm, an area of fields and orchards watered by the River Crane and, since the 1860s, bisected by the railway line.

Anon, *Main entrance of Twickenham Technical College and School of Art*, c.1937 (colour print on board, 1971, RUTC)

Teaching began at the College in September 1937. A three year full time junior course in general art studies for pupils at age 13+ and a more advanced senior art course for students at 16+ were begun. Part-time evening classes courses were provided in 'General Art', Sign Writing, Art Metalwork, Silversmithing, Jewellery, Bookbinding, Photography and Photo-lithography. The Art Department produced a brochure for the ceremonial opening of the College in March 1938 described as being 'composed in the Bembo series on "Monotype" machines and printed on the Michele Two-Revolution Press'.

The Art School shared with the other departments of the College the difficulties arising from war-time and post-war shortages and the constant changes in the structure of technical education, both locally and nationally, which took place

Drawing from the Antique, art class at Twickenham Technical Institute, 1938 (ill. C.W. Radcliffe, *Middlesex*, Evans Bros, 1939)

in the 1950s and 1960s. The establishment of a graphic design department in 1958, with Osmund Caine whom we have already mentioned as its inspirational head, was an important watershed. Brian Pearce wrote in 1972:

> Through exhibitions, excellent employment records, examination successes, the execution of murals for local schools and libraries, RSA Bursary successes, and active liaison with industry, the design courses at Twickenham have established a solid reputation, which attracts students from all over the country and abroad. [1]

Art students from the college have featured regularly in the annual RSA Student Design Awards Scheme, whose purpose since their inception in the 1920s has been to challenge professional designers-in-training to apply their skills to difficult social issues. While it was not felt either feasible or essentially relevant to the scope of the present study to document fully the college participation in this scheme, it was deemed appropriate to include some examples of the quality of student work which has won awards: these particular instances are taken from the RUTC archives.

---

[1] B. Pearce, *Twickenham College of Technology. The first thirty-five years 1937-1972* (Twickenham, 1973).

BELOW: David Hubball, RSA Student Design Award 1994 for packaging
BELOW RIGHT UPPER: Stuart Hall, RSA Student Design Award 1997 for postage stamps
BELOW RIGHT LOWER: Kevin Wright, RSA Student Design Award 1997 for graphics

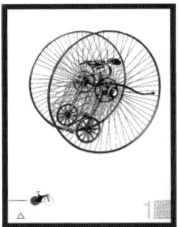

In 1991 Paul Torode was awarded The John Lewis Partnership Attachment Award worth £3,000 for his packaging project: his work was thought to be 'clean and professional', his presentation was described as very good and his portfolio said to reveal the breadth of his ability.

In 1994 David Hubball received the Shiseido Attachment Award, value £2,000, with his response to the packaging brief: the judges' report instanced his comprehensive research and stated that his 'designs for hand tools packaging emphasised the function of the tool itself, and were smart, appropriate and well produced in model form.'

In 1997 the college gained two awards; a travel award worth £900 to Kevin Wright for his entry in the graphics brief, his 'choice of images from both past and present illustrate innovation'; and further recognition in the form of a travel award worth £1,000 to Stuart Hall for his entry in the postage stamps brief, illustrating 'science, space, time and the unknown'. In 1999 Wayne Peach also received a travel award, worth £700, for his 'Fresher Coffee' promotion in the Design Council brief.

MUTALIB MAN

A believer in the use of *objets trouvés* and three dimensional and semi-sculptural forms, Mutalib Man (1949-) has won acclaim for his intensely personal works, where western and eastern influences, though known to the artist, are barely perceptible in a challenging albeit restrained response to the universal human condition. After attending the MARA Institute, Kuala Lumpur, in his native Malaysia from 1969-72 Man came to this country to study graphic reproduction technology at the London College of Printing in 1972. Until 1980 when he settled in Twickenham, he worked as a graphic designer, translator and printer in East Sussex. From 1988 to 1997 he conducted an art therapy group and worked as a carer at Centre 32 (Mind) in Twickenham. He contributed to numerous exhibitions and art festivals in Richmond, Frome and London. In 1998 he was artist in residence at the Rimbun Dahan Foundation, Selangor, Malaysia. In 2006 he was awarded the Celeste art prize and in 2009 his work *Sea Sauce* was shortlisted for the Jerwood Drawing Prize, Jerwood Space in London.

Mutalib Man (1949-) *Untitled,* wall sculpture with coconut 1995 (mixed media with coconut, 77.5 x 41 x 29.1 cm, National Art Gallery, Malaysia)

Sea Sauce 3 is a two-dimensional piece in Indian ink and oil on canvas measuring 54cm x 54 cm, which Man developed from a site specific work. 20 thin steel rods 10' in length, with ping pong balls attached at intervals, were planted among trees and shrubs, interacting with and becoming part of the surroundings. From this installation Man derived his *Sea Sauce* series. Over a continuing number of paintings and multimedia artworks he explores the interaction of lines –sometimes straight, sometimes curved–with dots –sometimes single, sometimes multiple– placed all over the canvas, the dots acting as

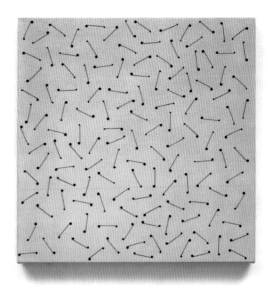

Mutalib Man (1949-), *Sea Sauce 3*, 2009
(mixed media, 54 x 54cm, private collection)

fulcrums upon which the lines balance; hence the initial name for the series of works was 'Sea Saws'. The final title *Sea Sauce* was chosen to suggest further interpretations by the viewer.

Like many abstract artists Mutalib is capable of producing figurative work but reluctant to do so because of his awareness of the baggage of art history. This sense of 'time past' is matched by a sense of place. He loves the quasi-industrial relics mixed with the 'Corot-like' poplars and natural grasses in the hinterland of his Mereway home. In 2004 as a homage to his locality he painted a view of All Saints Church in Campbell Road. Yet in the ochres and greys found in his abstract works, hints of the walls and pavements of Twickenham may be found, mixed with suggestions of the jungle leafage and temple openings of his homeland.

Man took British citizenship in 2008 and is also a regular visitor to his family and friends in Malaysia.[1]

---

[1] Catalogues of Redison Tanjury Rhu Collection, Langkawi, Malaysia (2001), and Frome Art Festival, 2008.

EPILOGUE

21st century interpretations of Turner's riverside

As David Allan perceptively observes in his introduction, the teaching and learning of art in the shadow of Twickenham's historic artistic legacy has, over the years, added both inspiration and creativity to the work emanating from the students of this college. The river in particular has provided a regular focus for their artistic expression; their response, in media covering all the disciplines of the college's School of Art, has ranged from the figurative to the abstract, the conceptual to the specific, the emotional to the mechanical.

We hope that you will enjoy the recent interpretations of the river included in this epilogue. Invited to make their own responses to the river, our students have in their own way captured moments both fixed in time and imbued with the fluidity imparted by its history.

The history of art is the history of boundaries proposed, erected, observed and broken. Turner ran the full gamut of these experiences; in the same way I hope that the School's offerings of these 21st century interpretations of the Thames at Twickenham do justice to that long tradition. Turner, and his fellow local residents across the centuries, would, I hope, approve of what today's students have brought to the river their predecessors so loved and painted.

Mary B. Eighteen
Programme Manager, Art and Design, Richmond upon Thames College

Hugh Craig, *River View, Twickenham*, photograph, 2010

Graphic Communication students: sketches from Twickenham Embankment, 2010

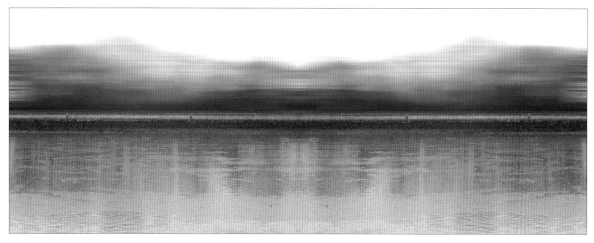

Hugh Craig, *Riverside inspired by Gursky,* manipulated photograph, 2010

Ella Montgomery-Smith, *Eel Pie Island*, ink on engraved aluminium sheet, 21cm x 29.5cm, 2010

Isabel Karpel-McCallum, *Water study*, water and body colour, sketchbook, 2010

Victoria Bickford-Sawking, *Water pattern*, textile, batik with applied beads, 2010

APPENDIX I

Abbreviations

USED IN CAPTIONS, NOTES AND LISTS

ARA   Associate of the Royal Academy
ARCA   Associate of the Royal College of Art
BOTLHS   Borough of Twickenham Local History Society
FRSA   Fellow of the Royal Society of Arts
FSA   Fellow of the Society of Antiquaries
LBRUT   London Borough of Richmond upon Thames
NPG   National Portrait Gallery
ODNB   Oxford Dictionary of National Biography
RA   Royal Academy [Academician]
RCA   Royal College of Art
[R]SA   [Royal] Society for the encouragement of Arts, Manufactures and Commerce [after 1908]
RUTC   Richmond upon Thames College (formerly Twickenham College of Technology and School of Art)
RWS   Royal Watercolour Society
TVAC   Thames Valley Arts Club
WSG   William Shipley Group for RSA History

USED IN THE LISTS OF ARTISTS

Arch	Architect	MSIA	Member of the Society of Industrial Artists
Am	Amateur		
Bk	Book illustrator	Pho	Photographer
C	Ceiling and wall painter	Post	Poster artist
Cr	Craftsman	Pp	Portrait painter
Eng	Engraver	PRA	President of the Royal Academy
F	Flower painter		
G	Garden designer	Res	Resident
Gl	Stained glass worker/designer	RDI	Royal Designer for Industry
Loc	Work done in the locality	Sc	Sculptor
Lp	Landscape painter	Stop	Stopover
Lv	Local views	T	Teacher
M	Miniaturist	Text	Textile designer
Mm	Mixed media user	W	Watercolourist

APPENDIX 2

Lists of artists

Entries for amateurs are printed in italics

GENERAL LIST

♦ ADAM, James (1732-94). Arch; Stop; Hampton Court, c.1768 (*see also under* Adam, Robert)

♦ ADAM, Robert (1728-92), MP FRS FSA. Arch; Stop; Syon House, Twickenham Park, Strawberry Hill, Hampton, c.1760-72

ANGUS, William (1752-1831). Eng; Lv; Twickenham Park, 1795

★♦ ANSBACH, Elizabeth, Margravine (1750-1828). Pp; Stop; Strawberry Hill

ARBUTHNOT, George (fl.1780). Awarded silver palette for drawing, 1780. Res; Rev.L.M. Stretch's Academy, Bath House, Twickenham

ARCHER, Thomas (c.1668-1743). Arch; Sc; Loc; Stop; Hampton Church, c.1731

ATHALIN, Laurent, General (fl.1814-17). Lp; Lv; Res; Ferry House, Twickenham, c.1814-17

BALL, William (1853-1917). Eng; Lp; Stop; Twickenham Ferry before 1917

BARNARD, George (1815-90). Lp; Lv; Marble Hill Cottage, c.1831

BARNES, Ernest William (1880-1966). Eng; Pp; Poster artist; Res; Elmfield Avenue, Teddington, c.1930-60

BARRETT, George, jnr (fl.1800-24). Lp; Lv; Twickenham River View, c.1820

BARROW, Joseph Charles (b.c.1770-1804). Lp; Lv; T; Stop; Strawberry Hill; near St Mary's Church Twickenham, c.1789

BECKLES WILLSON, Anthony (1928-), B.Arch ARIBA FSA. Arch; Sc; Res; Twickenham Green and Pope's Avenue, 1980-

♦ BOYDELL, John (1720-1804). Eng; Lv; Stop; Twickenham, 1753

BROWN, Mortimer (1874-1966), RBS. Sc; Stop; Radnor Gardens, Twickenham, 1921

BROWNE, Hablot Knight (1815-82). Bk; Stop; Twickenham, c.1857

♦ BURY, Adrian (1891-1991), RWS. LP, W; LV; Book illustrator; Res; Church Street, Old Isleworth, c.1930-60

CAINE, Osmund (1914-2004). Lp; Lv; T; Stained glass designer; Res; Kingston Hill, 1948-2004

CANALETTO, Giovanni Antonio (1697-1768). Lp; Lv; Stop; Syon House, 1749

CATTERSON-SMITH, Isobel, Miss (daughter of Robert) (fl.1932), TVAC. F; Stop; TVAC exhibition 1932

CATTERSON-SMITH, Robert (fl.1932), TVAC. Pp; Stop; TVAC exhibition 1932

CHALON, John James (1778-1854), RA. Lp; Lv; W; Stop; River by Orleans House, c.1840

♦ CHAMBERS, Sir William (1726-96), RA. Arch; Res; Whitton Place, c.1781-96

★ CLENNELL, Luke (fl.1806). Eng; Res; Twickenham Common, 1806

CONNARD, Philip (1876-1958), RA TVAC. Lp; Lv; Res; Cholmondeley Lodge, Richmond, c.1908-58

COOKE, William (fl.1807). Eng; Lp; Stop; Pope's House, 1807

COOPER, Alfred W. (fl.1862-1903). Pp; Lp; W; Book illustrator; Stop; Banks of Rivers Thames and Crane, Twickenham, 1862, c.1880

COROT, Jean Baptiste Camille (1796-1875). Lp; Stop; Richmond and Twickenham Riverside, 1862

CUNARD, Laura Charlotte [née Haliburton], Mrs (1824-1910). W; Res; Orleans House, Twickenham, c.1851-1910

CUNEO, Terence (1907-96), TVAC. Pp; C; Stop; (TVAC exhibition, 1949)

CURTIS, John (fl.1782-c.1808). Lp; Res; Manor House, Twickenham, c.1783-1808

DAMER, Anne Seymour Conway, The Hon. Mrs (1748-1828). Sc; Res; Strawberry Hill and York House, Twickenham, c.1790-1828

DEARE, John (1759-98). Sc; Stop; Whitton, c.1783

♦ DELAMOTTE, Philip Henry (1821-89). Pho; Lp; T; Lv; Res; Belmont Place, c.1850-67; 11 Clifden Road, c.1867; Grosvenor Lodge, 1867-

DE WINT, Peter (1784-1849). Lp; Lv; Stop; Garrick's Villa, Hampton, c.1850

♦ *DIAMOND, Hugh Welch (1808-86). Pho; Loc; Res; Twickenham House, c.1858-86*

DRING, Lillian, Mrs [née Welch] (1908-98), ARCA. T; Poster artist and textile designer; Res; Teddington, 1940-98

FANELLI, Francesco (fl.1608-65). Sc; Stop; Privy Garden, Hampton Court, c.1610

FRASER, Eric (1902-82). Eng; T; Poster artist; Res; Penn's Place, Hampton, c.1935-82

FRASER, Geoffrey M., Revd (1929-). Mural painter; Res; Penn's Place, Hampton, c.1952-c.1970

FRENCH, John Richardson Lowndes, 2nd Earl of Ypres, Rt Hon. (1881-1953), JP. TVAC. W; Lp; Res; Ivy House, Hampton Court, c.1925-53

FULLWOOD, John (1854-1931), FSA. Eng; Lp; Lv; Res; Tennyson Avenue, Twickenham, c.1920-31

GARVERY, Auguste (fl.1815). Lp; Lv; W; Stop; Orleans House, c.1815

GAVEY, Edith (fl.1906). F; Lp; Res; Hampton, c.1906

GEDDES, Margaret (1914-98). Pp; Res; 'Old Coach House', Blandford Road, Teddington, c.1960-97

GLOVER, Moses (1601-c.1635). Arch; Lp; Lv; Res; Isleworth, c.1622-35

♦ GLUCK, Felix (1923-81), MSIA. Eng; Book illustrator; Res; 72 Northcote Road, Twickenham, c.1956-81

GOSSELIN, Joshua (1739-1813). Lp; W; Lv; Stop; Whitton, c.1791

GRANT, Duncan (1885-1978). Lp; Lv; Textile designer; Stop; Grosvenor House, Grosvenor Road, Twickenham, 1924-c.1940

GULLIVER, Richard (d.c.1622). Lp; Pp; Res; Isleworth before 1622

HECKEL, Augustin (1690-1770). Lp; W; Lv; Res; Richmond, 1746-70

♦ *HILDITCH, George (1803-57). Lp; Pho; Lv; Stop; Montpelier Row, Twickenham, c.1813-17*

♦ *HILDITCH, John Bracebridge (fl.1890-1920) JP. Pho; Pat; Lv; Res; Asquith House, Richmond, c.1898*

HILDITCH, Richard Henry (1803-73). Lp; Stop; Montpelier Row, Twickenham, c.1813-19

HILLIARD, Nicholas (1547-1619). M; Pp; Stop; Metal works at Isleworth, c.1600

HOFLAND, Thomas Christopher (1787-1843). Lp; Book illustrator; T; Res; Montpelier Row, Twickenham, c.1815

HOLBEIN, Hans, the younger (1497-1543). Pp; Eng; Stop; Hampton Court, c.1536

HOLLAR, Wenceslaus (1607-77). Eng; Lp; Stop; Hampton Court, c.1647

HORNE, Galyow (fl.1690-1702). Gl; Stop; Hampton Court, c.1690-1702

HOWARD, William (1800-50). Lp; Lv; Stop; Twickenham Parish Church, c.1830

♦ HUDSON, Thomas (1701-79). Pp; Res; Cross Deep, Twickenham, 1753-79

HUMPHRY, Ozias (1742-1810). M; Pp; Lp; Stop; Pope's Villa, Twickenham
        Riverside, c.1764; Strawberry Hill, c.1764-80

HUNT, William Henry (1790-1864). Lp; W; Stop; Twickenham, 1806

IRONSIDE, Edward (c1736-1803). W; Lv; Res; 6 Sion Row, Twickenham, 1763-77;
        Spackman's Buildings, King Street, Twickenham, 1778-9

*JARNAC, C.R.de Rohan Chabot, Comte de (fl.c.1806-17). Lv;W; Res; Sion Row,
        Twickenham, c.1817*

JERVAS, Charles (1675-1739). Pp; Res; Elm Lodge, Hampton, 1782-89

♦ *KINGSLEY, Sutton (d.1976), TVAC. Lp; Stop; TVAC meetings c.1970-76*

KNELLER, Sir Godfrey (1646-1721). Pp; Res; Whitton, 1709-23

LAGUERRE, Louis (1663-1723). Loc; Ceiling and wall painter; Stop; Whitton,
        c.1709

LEAR, Edward (1812-88). Bk; Eng; W; Stop; Strawberry Hill, 1857

LELY, Peter, Sir (1618-80). Pp; Stop; Syon Park House, 1647

LINDO, Francis (fl.1761-70). Pp; Loc; Res; Isleworth, c.1760-70

LINNELL, John (1792-1882). Lp; Stop; Twickenham, 1806

MAN, Mutalib (1949-). Mm; T; Res; Mereway Road, Twickenham, c.1980-

MARLOW, William (1740-1813). Lp; Res; Manor House, Twickenham, 1783-1813

*MASON, J. (fl.1828). Sc; Res; Twickenham, 1828

MICKLEM, Bridget (1963-). Pp; Res; Hampton (c.1980-)

♦ MILLET, Lucy Constance Marion (fl.c.1880-1948). Eng; Lp; Lv; T; Res; 11
        Seymour Road, Hampton Wick, c.1906; Gomer House, Lower Teddington
        Road, Hampton Wick, c.1920-47

MUNTZ, Johann Heinrich (fl.1755-75). Cr; Eng; Lp; Lv; Res; Strawberry Hill,
        c.1755-9

NEEDHAM, James (fl.1530s). Cr; Res; Hampton Court, c.1532

*NISBET, Ethel, Mrs (fl.1889-1900). F; Lv; Book illustrator; Res; Laurel Lodge, Heath
        Road, Twickenham, c.1900*

NIGHTINGALE, Paula, Mrs (1937-). Bk; Lp; Mm; T; W; Stop; Hampton Riverside,
        2000-09

OLIVER, Isaac (c.1565-1617). M; Pp; Res; Isleworth, c.1606

OLIVER, Peter (1594-1646). M; Pp; Res; Isleworth, c.1616

*♦ PARS, William (1742-82). Lp; T; Stop; Pope's Villa, Twickenham. Riverside,
        Strawberry Hill, 1772

PAYNE, William (1760-1830). Lp; Lv; T; W; Stop; Kneller Hall, Whitton, c.1800

PEEL, Carli (fl.1900). Book illustrator; Res; Twickenham, 1900

PETHER, Henry (1800-80). Lp; Lv; Stop; Eel Pie Island, c.1835

PHIPSON, Edward Arthur (1854-1931). Lp; Stop; Bell Lane, Twickenham, 1904

PINGRET, Edouard (1788-1875). Eng; Bk; Pp; Stop; Orleans House, Twickenham,
        1844

POPE, Alexander (1688-1744). G; Lp; Lv; Res; Twickenham Riverside, 1719-44

*PRINSEP, Emily Rebecca (fl.1820-50). Lp; Lv; Panorama of Twickenham from Richmond
        Hill, c.1840*

♦ REYNOLDS, Joshua, Sir (1723-92) PRA. Lv; Pp; Res; Isleworth, Twickenham,
        Richmond, c.1759-1785)

RICCI, Sebastiano (1659-1734). C; Lp; Lv; Stop; Richmond Lodge riverbank c.1727

RYSBRACK, John Michael (1694-1770). Sc; Stop; St Mary's Church, Twickenham, c.1750

♦ SANDBY, Paul (1725-1808). Lp; Lv; T; Stop; Strawberry Hill, c.1769

SHACKLETON, William, TVAC. Pp, Lp, Stop; TVAC exhibition 1932

SCOTT, Samuel (1702-72). Lp; Lv; Book illustrator; Res; near Strawberry Hill, 1748; Manor House, Twickenham, 1758-65

SEYMOUR, Edward (d.1757). Pp; Res; Twickenham, c.1716-57 (Syon Row 1722)

SHAW, Huntingdon (1659-1710). Cr; Res; nr Hampton Court, c.1700-10

SISLEY, Alfred (1839-99). Lp; Stop; Hampton riverside 1874

SPYERS, John (c.1720-98). C; Eng; Lv; Res; Grosvenor House, nr London Road, Twickenham, c.1790-98

STACEY, Richard (fl.1690-1702). Cr; Res; Bricklayer at Hampton Court, c.1690-1702

STOKES, James (fl.1841-63). Lp; Lv; Res; Isleworth, c.1841-8

STOKES, William (fl.1841-63). Lp; Res; Isleworth, c.1841-63

STOREY, Jill, Mrs (1950-). Lp; Mm; T; W; Lv; Book illustrator; Res; Copthall Gardens, Twickenham, 1980-

TABOR, Hélène, TVAC. Pp; Res; Teddington (wife of Hugh Tabor), c.1906

TABOR, Hugh, TVAC (fl.1906). Lp; Res; Teddington, c.1906

TAYLOR, Simon (c.1743-96). F; Stop; Kew, c.1758-60

THURSTON, John (fl.1690-1762). Cr; Res; Plasterer at Hampton Court, c.1690-1762

TILLEMANS, Peter (1684-1734). Lp; Lv; Res; Richmond Hill, c.1730-34

★ TURNER, Joseph Mallord William (1775-1851), RA. Bk; Lp; Lv; Res; Sandycombe Lodge, Twickenham, c.1810-26

★ *TWINING, Elizabeth (1805-89). F; Res; Dial House, Twickenham, c.1866-89*

VARLEY, John (1778-1842). Lp; Lv; T; Stop; Twickenham, 1806

VELLACOTT, Avril (1941-). Sc; T; Res; Elmfield Avenue, Teddington, c.1962-

VERRIO, Antonio (c.1639-1707). Pp; Ceiling and wall painter; G; Res; Hampton Court, c.1700-07

★ *WALDEGRAVE, Laura, The Rt Hon Lady (1760-1814). W; Stop; Strawberry Hill, c.1780*

★ *WALPOLE, Caroline, The Hon Miss. W; Res; Isleworth, c.1780-81*

♦ *WALPOLE, Horace, 4th Earl of Orford (1717-91). Arch; Bk; G; Res; Strawberry Hill, c.1750-92*

WARD, Enoch (1859-1922). Eng; Lp; W; Book illustrator; Res; 'Walnut Tree Cottage', Old Castle Wharf, Hampton Wick, c.1910-22

WAY, Thomas R. (fl.c.1880-c.1900). Eng; Lp; Book illustrator; Stop; Church Street and King Street, Twickenham, c.1900

WILSON, Richard (1714-82). Lp; Lv; Stop; Isleworth, c.1759-60

♦ WOOLLETT, William (1735-85). Lp; Lv; Stop; Whitton, c.1757

WREN, Christopher, Sir (1632-1723). Arch; Res; Old Court House, Hampton, c.1708-23

ZOFFANY, Johann (1733-1810), RA. Pp; Loc; Stop; Hampton (Garrick's Villa), 1762

♦ Society of Arts Member
★ Society of Arts prize winner

CHRONOLOGICAL LIST

In birth order if known, or by earliest listed date

Holbein, Hans, the younger
Needham, James
Hilliard, Nicholas
Oliver, Nicholas
Oliver, Peter
Glover, Moses
Hollar, Wenceslaus
Fanelli, Francesco
Lely, Sir Peter
Gulliver, Richard
Wren, Sir Christopher
Verrio, Antonio
Kneller, Sir Godfrey
Ricci, Sebastiano
Shaw, Huntingdon
Laguerre, Louis
Archer, Thomas
Jervas, Charles
Pope, Alexander
Tillemans, Peter
Heckel, Augustin
Stacey, Richard
Thurston, John
Horne, Galyow
Rysbrack, John Michael
Canaletto, Giovanni Antonio de
Hudson, Thomas
Scott, Samuel
Wilson, Richard
Walpole, Horace, 4th Earl of Orford
Boydell, John
Spyers, John
Reynolds, Sir Joshua
Sandby, Paul
Chambers, Sir William
Adam, James
Zoffany, Johann
Woollett, William
Ironside, Edward
Gosselin, Joshua
Marlow, William
Humphry, Ozias
Pars, William
Taylor, Simon

Damer, Anne Seymour Conway, The Hon
Ansbach, Elizabeth, Margravine
Angus, William
Muntz, Johann Heinrich
Seymour, Edward
Deare, John
Payne, William
Curtis, John
Arbuthnot, George
Waldegrave, Laura, The Rt Hon Lady
Lindo, Francis
Adam, Robert
Barrett, George, jnr
Turner, Joseph Mallord William
Chalon, John James
Cooke, William Bernard
Walpole, Caroline, The Hon Miss
De Wint, Peter
Hofland, Thomas Christopher
Pingret, Edouard
Corot, Jean Baptiste Camille
Barrett, George, jnr
Howard, William
Pether, Henry
Hilditch, George
Hilditch, Richard Henry
Twining, Elizabeth
Clennell, Luke
Diamond, Hugh Welch
Lear, Edward
Athalin, Laurent
Browne, Hablot Knight
Barnard, George
Garvery, Auguste
Jarnac, C.R. de Rohan Chabot, Comte de
Prinsep, Emily Rebecca
Delamotte, Philip Henry
Cunard, Laura Charlotte
Mason, J.
Sisley, Alfred
Stokes, James

Stokes, William
Ball, William
Ward, Enoch
Fullwood, John
Phipson, Edward Arthur
Cooper, Alfred W.
Brown, Mortimer
Connard, Philip
Millet, Lucy Constance Marion
Barnes, Ernest William
Way, Thomas R.
French, John Richardson Lowndes
Grant, Duncan
Nisbet, Ethel
Hilditch, John Bracebridge
Bury, Adrian
Peel, Carli
Fraser, Eric
Gavey, Edith
Tabor, Hélène
Cuneo, Terence
Dring, Lillian
Caine, Osmund
Geddes, Margaret
Gluck, Felix
Beckles Willson, Anthony
Vellacott, Avril
Fraser, Geoffrey M.
Catterson-Smith, Isobel
Catterson-Smith, Robert
Shackleton, William
Nightingale, Paula
Man, Mutalib
Storey, Jill
Micklem, Bridget
Kingsley, Sutton

OCCUPATIONAL CATEGORIES

Architects
Adam, James
Adam, Robert

Archer, Thomas
Beckles Willson, Anthony

Walpole, Horace
Wren, Sir Christopher

Craftsmen
Muntz, Johann Heinrich
Needham, James
Ricci, Sebastiano

Shaw, Huntingdon
Spyers, John
Stacey, Richard

Thurston, John

Engravers
Angus, William
Ball, William
Barnes, Ernest William
Boydell, John
Browne, Hablot Knight
Clennell, Luke

Cooke, William Bernard
Fraser, Eric
Fullwood, John
Gluck, Felix
Holbein, Hans
Hollar, Wenceslaus

Lear, Edward
Millet, Lucy Constance Marion
Muntz, Johann Heinrich
Pingret, Edouard
Spyers, John
Way, Thomas R.

Landscape painters
Athalin, Laurent
Ball, William
Barnard, George
Barrett, George, jnr
Barrow, Joseph Charles
Bury, Adrian
Caine, Osmund
Canaletto, Giovanni Antonio de
Chalon, John James
Connard, Philip
Cooper, Alfred W.
Corot, Jean Baptiste Camille
Cuneo, Terence
Curtis, John
De Wint, Peter
French, John R. Lowndes
Fullwood, John
Garvery, Auguste
Gavey, Edith
Geddes, Margaret

Glover, Moses
Gosselin, Joshua
Grant, Duncan
Gulliver, Richard
Heckel, Augustin
Hilditch, George
Hilditch, Richard Henry
Hofland, Thomas Christopher
Hollar, Wenceslaus
Howard, William
Humphry, Ozias
Hunt, William Henry
Kingsley, Sutton
Linnell, John
Marlow, William
Millet, Lucy Constance Marion
Muntz, Johann Heinrich
Nightingale, Paula
Pars, William
Payne, William

Pether, Henry
Phipson, Edward Arthur
Pope, Alexander
Prinsep, Emily Rebecca
Ricci, Sebastiano
Sandby, Paul
Scott, Samuel
Shackleton, William
Sisley, Alfred
Stokes, James
Stokes, William
Storey, Jill
Tabor, Hugh
Tillemans, Peter
Turner, Joseph Mallord William
Varley, John
Ward, Enoch
Way, Thomas R.
Wilson, Richard
Woollett, William

Miniaturists
Hilliard, Nicholas
Humphry, Ozias

Oliver, Isaac
Oliver, Peter

Wilson, Richard
Woollett, William

Mixed media users
Geddes, Margaret
Man, Mutalib

Nightingale, Paula
Storey, Jill

Photographers
Delamotte, Philip Henry
Diamond, Hugh Welch

Hilditch, George
Hilditch, John Bracebridge

Portrait painters
Ansbach, Elizabeth, Margravine
Barnes, Ernest William
Catterson-Smith, Robert
Cooper, Alfred W.
Geddes, Margaret
Gulliver, Richard
Hilliard, Nicholas
Holbein, Hans

Hudson, Thomas
Humphry, Ozias
Jervas, Charles
Kneller, Sir Godfrey
Lely, Sir Peter
Lindo, Francis
Micklem, Bridget
Oliver, Isaac

Oliver, Peter
Pingret, Edouard
Reynolds, Sir Joshua
Seymour, Edward
Shackleton, William
Tabor, Hélène
Verrio, Antonio
Zoffany, Johann

Sculptors
Beckles Willson, Anthony
Brown, Mortimer
Damer, Anne Seymour Conway

Deare, John
Fanelli, Francesco
Mason, J.

Rysbrack, John Michael
Vellacott, Avril

Watercolourists
Bury, Adrian
Cunard, Laura
French, John R. Lowndes
Garvey, Auguste
Gosselin, Joshua
Heckel, Augustin
Hunt, William Henry

Ironside, Edward
Jarnac, Comte de
Lear, Edward
Nightingale, Paula
Nisbet, Ethel
Payne, William
Phipson, Edward Arthur

Sandby, Paul
Storey, Jill
Turner, Joseph Mallord William
Waldegrave, Laura
Walpole, Caroline
Ward, Enoch

ARTISTS WHO RESIDED IN THE AREA

Arbuthnot, George
Athalin, Laurent
Barnes, Ernest William
Beckles Willson, Anthony
Bury, Adrian
Caine, Osmund
Chambers, Sir William
Clennell, Luke
Connard, Philip
Cunard, Laura Charlotte
Curtis, John
Damer, Anne Seymour Conway
Delamotte, Philip Henry
Diamond, Hugh Welch
Dring, Lilian
Fraser, Eric
Fraser, Geoffrey M.
French, John R. Lowndes
Fullwood, John
Gavey, Edith
Geddes, Margaret
Glover, Moses

Gluck, Felix
Gulliver, Richard
Heckel, Augustin
Hilditch, John Bracebridge
Hofland, Thomas Christopher
Hudson, Thomas
Ironside, Edward
Jarnac, Comte de
Jervas, Charles
Kneller, Sir Godfrey
Man, Mutalib
Marlow, William
Mason, J.
Millet, Lucy Constance Marion
Micklem, Bridget
Muntz, Johann Heinrich, Mrs
Needham, James
Nisbet, Ethel
Oliver, Issac
Oliver, Peter
Peel, Carli
Pope, Alexander

Reynolds, Joshua
Scott, Samuel
Seymour, Edward
Shaw, Huntingdon
Spyers, John
Stacey, Richard
Stokes, James
Stokes, William
Storey, Jill
Tabor, Hélène
Tabor, Hugh
Thurston, John
Tillemans, Peter
Turner, Joseph Mallord William
Twining, Elizabeth
Vellacott, Avril
Verrio, Antonio
Walpole, Caroline
Walpole, Horace
Ward, Enoch
Wren, Sir Christopher

ARTISTS WHO VISITED THE AREA

Adam, James
Adam, Robert
Ansbach, Elizabeth, Margravine
Archer, Thomas
Ball, William
Barrow, Joseph Charles
Boydell, John
Brown, Mortimer
Browne, Hablot Knight
Canaletto, Giovanni Antonio de
Catterson-Smith, Isobel
Catterson-Smith, Robert
Chalon, John James
Cooke, William Bernard
Cooper, Alfred W.
Corot, Jean Baptiste Camille
Cuneo, Terence
Deare, John

De Wint, Peter
Fanelli, Francesco
Garvey, Auguste
Gosselin, Joshua
Grant, Duncan
Hilditch, George
Hilditch, Richard Henry
Hilliard, Nicholas
Holbein, Hans
Hollar, Wenceslaus
Horne, Galyow
Howard, William
Humphry, Ozias
Kingsley, Sutton
Laguerre, Louis
Lear, Edward
Lely, Sir Peter
Lindo, Francis

Nightingale, Paula
Pars, William
Payne, William
Pether, Henry
Phipson, Edward Arthur
Pingret, Edouard
Ricci, Sebastiano
Rysbrack, John Michael
Sandby, Paul
Shackleton, William
Sisley, Alfred
Taylor, Simon
Waldegrave, Laura
Way, Thomas R.
Wilson, Richard
Woollett, William
Zoffany, Johann

TEDDINGTON ARTISTS GROUP

founded 1990

CLARK, Sue. F; Eng; Mm
DAVIDSON, Lisa. Cr; Works in ceramics
DEVENISH, Peter (d.2008). Eng; Pho
EATWELL, Christine. Eng; T
FARNHAM, Jane. Cr; Jewellery designer
KNUTT, Liz. Lp; Exhibitor RA 1997
RIBBANS, Hugh. Eng; Mm; Wood and lino cut engraver
RIBBANS, Sue. Eng; Mm; Lino cut printer
VELLACOTT, Avril (*see General List*). Sc; T
WEBB, Ewa Wnek. Eng; Mm; W; Exhibitor RA 1996

APPENDIX 3

Locations

BEFORE 1700

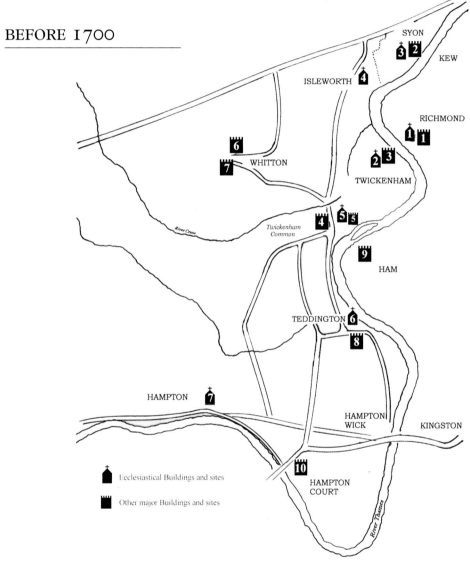

ECCLESIASTICAL BUILDINGS AND SITES

Abbey of St Augustin (Carthusian at Sheen)	1
Monastery of St Saviour and St Bridget of Syon (1415)	2
Monastery of St Saviour and St Bridget of Syon (1426)	3
All Souls' Church, Isleworth	4
St Mary's Church, Twickenham	5
St Mary's Church, Teddington	6
St Mary's Church, Hampton	7

OTHER MAJOR BUILDINGS AND SITES

Richmond (formerly Sheen) Palace	1
Syon House	2
Twickenham Park House	3
Twickenham Manor	4
York House	5
Whitton Manor	6
Kneller Hall	7
Teddington Place	8
Ham House	9
Hampton Court	10

BEFORE 1800

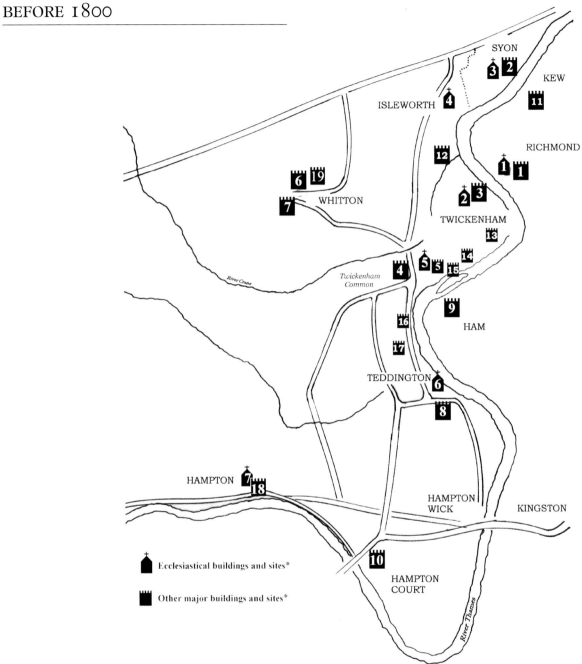

ECCLESIASTICAL BUILDINGS AND SITES

Abbey of St Augustin (Carthusian at Sheen)*	1
Monastery of St Saviour and St Bridget of Syon (1415)*	2
Monastery of St Saviour and St Bridget of Syon (1426)*	3
All Souls' Church, Isleworth	4
St Mary's Church, Twickenham	5
St Mary's Church, Teddington	6
St Mary's Church, Hampton	7

OTHER MAJOR BUILDINGS AND SITES

Richmond (formerly Sheen) Palace	1	Kew Palace	11
Syon House	2	Gordon House	12
Twickenham Park House	3	Cambridge Park	13
Twickenham Manor	4	Marble Hill House	14
York House	5	Orleans House	15
Whitton Manor	6	Pope's Villa and Grotto	16
Kneller Hall	7	Strawberry Hill	17
Teddington Place	8	Garrick's Villa and Temple	18
Ham House	9	Whitton Dene	19
Hampton Court	10		

BEFORE 1900

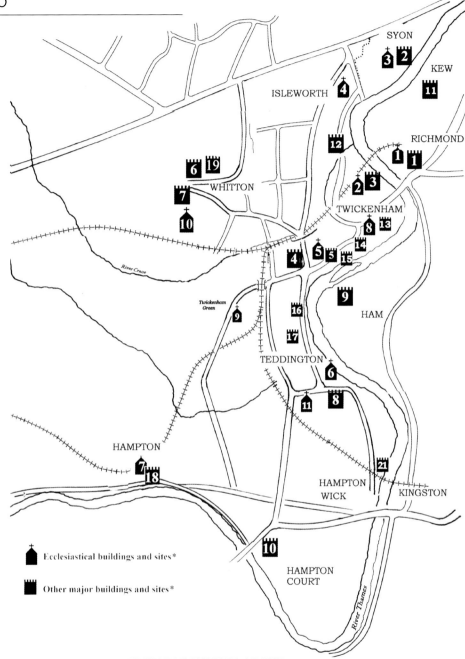

ECCLESIASTICAL BUIDINGS AND SITES

Abbey of St Augustine (Carthusian at Sheen)*	1
Monastery of St Saviour and St Bridget of Syon (1415)*	2
Monastery of St Saviour and St Bridget of Syon (1426)*	3
All Souls' Church Isleworth	4
St Mary's Church ,Twickenham	5
St Mary's Church, Teddington	6
St Mary's Church, Hampton	7
St Stephen's Church, Twickenham	8
Holy Trinity Church, Twickenham	9
St Philip and St James's, Whitton	10
St Peter and St Paul's, Teddington	11

OTHER MAJOR BUILDINGS AND SITES

Richmond (formerly Sheen) Palace	1	Gordon House	12
Syon House	2	Cambridge Park	13
Twickenham Park House*	3	Marble Hill House	14
Twickenham Manor*	4	Orleans House	15
York House	5	Pope's Villa and Grotto	16
Whitton Manor*	6	Strawberry Hill	17
Kneller Hall	7	Garrick's Villa and Temple	18
Teddington Place	8	Whitton Dene*	19
Ham House	9	Turner's Villa	20
Hampton Court	10	Normansfield	21
Kew Palace	11		

AFTER 1900

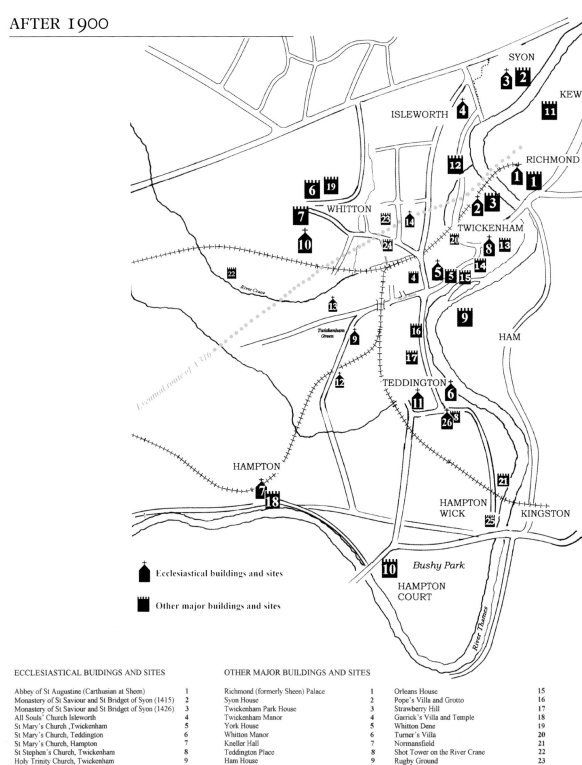

APPENDIX 4

Collections and Galleries in the area

THE ARCHITECT'S GALLERY

69-70 Broad Street, Teddington TW11 9QZ. Tel. 020 8977 2175.
www.thearchitectsgallery.com. Purpose built structure opened in 2008 for exhibiting
works by local artists and others: holds arts classes for adults and children.

CHURCHES

The churches indicated on the maps contain monuments and fittings by artists and
craftsmen of various periods and often display paintings and prints and photographs.
Access is generally available through the Church Wardens or at advertised service
times.

HAMPTON COURT PALACE

East Molesey, Surrey KT6 9AU. Tel 0844 482 7777.
www.hrp.org.uk/hamptoncourtpalace. Numerous views of the Palace and grounds
from the 16th century onwards are on display or in store.

HOUNSLOW LOCAL STUDIES LIBRARY

CentreSpace, Treaty Centre, Hounslow TW3 1ES. Tel 0845 456 2800.
www.hounslow.info/libraries/localstudies. Maintains and displays views of the
Isleworth area.

KINGSTON MUSEUM

Wheatfield Road, Kingston-upon-Thames KT1 2PS. Tel 020 8547 6460.
www.kingston.gov.uk/museum. The museum houses works by members of the
Thames Valley Arts Club (founded 1906)

LANDMARK ARTS CENTRE

Ferry Road, Teddington TW11 9NN. Tel 030 8977 7558.
www.landmarkartscentre.org. This is in the redundant Victorian Gothic Church of
St Alban the Martyr (built 1887-89, with some medieval glass windows) and used for
exhibitions by local art and photographic societies.

LONDON WILDLIFE TRUST

The Shot Tower, Crane Park. Tel 020 901 2334.
http://wildcrane.users.btopenworld.com. Houses early views of the Shot Tower and
the vicinity.

MARBLE HILL HOUSE

Richmond Road, Twickenham TW1 2NL. Tel 020 8892 5115.
www.english-heritage.org.uk/server.show/nav.12809. Henrietta Howard's Palladian
villa now owned by English Heritage. Displays early views of the house and grounds.

ORLEANS HOUSE GALLERY

Riverside, Twickenham TW1 3DJ. Tel 020 8831 6000.
www.richmond.gov.uk/orleans_house_gallery. Maintains and displays the Richmond
Borough Art Collections of over 2100 works originally from the Ionides Bequest of
1962 and later donations and acquisitions.

RICHMOND ADULT COMMUNITY COLLEGE

Clifden Road, Twickenham TW1 4LT; Parkshot Centre, Richmond TW9 2RE.
Tel 020 8891 5907. www.racc.ac.uk/ The Art Department holds regular exhibitions
of students' work.

RICHMOND LOCAL STUDIES LIBRARY (LBRUT)

Old Town Hall, Whittaker Avenue, Richmond TW9 1TP. Tel 020 8332 6820.
www.richmond.gov.uk/home/leisure_and_culture/local_history_and_heritage/local_
studies_collection.htm. Stores and maintains unframed items from the Borough Art
Collection.

RICHMOND MUSEUM

Old Town Hall, Whittaker Avenue, Richmond TW9 1TP. Tel 020 8332 1114.
www.museumofrichmond.com. Independent accredited museum partly supported
by LBRUT. Holds permanent collection of artefacts and has regular exhibitions.

RICHMOND UPON THAMES COLLEGE

Egerton Road, Twickenham TW2 7SJ. Tel 020 8607 8000. www.rutc.ac.uk.
Paintings and photographs by students are displayed throughout the building.

RIVERSIDE GALLERY

Old Town Hall, Whittaker Avenue, Richmond TW9 1TP. Tel 020 8831 6000.
www.richmond.gov.uk/home/leisure_and_culture/arts/riverside_gallery.htm.
Exhibits mixed media displays by local artists.

SANDYCOMBE LODGE

Sandycombe Road, Twickenham TW1 2LR. www.friendsofturnershouse.org.uk.
The villa built and designed by J.M.W. Turner, 1812, and since 2005 maintained by the
Sandycombe Lodge Trust houses a collection of Turner related books and engravings.

STABLES GALLERY

Orleans House Gallery, Riverside, Twickenham TW1 3DJ. Tel 020 8831 6000.
www.richmond.gov.uk/home/leisure_and_culture/arts/the_stables_gallery.htm.
The former stable block at Orleans House converted into a gallery and used to display
works by living local artists.

STRAWBERRY HILL

268 Waldegrave Road, Twickenham TW1 4ST. www.friendsofstrawberryhill.org.
Horace Walpole's 18th century 'Gothick' home maintained by the Strawberry Hill
Trust. Houses many early views of the house and grounds.

TEDDINGTON LIBRARY

Waldegrave Road, Twickenham TW11 8NY. Tel 020 8977 1284.
email: teddington.library@richmond.gov.uk. The 1906 Carnegie Library building
originally contained a portrait of Hugh Tabor, TVAC, now in the Borough Art
Collection. A bust by Avril Vellacott of Noel Coward, presented in 2000 by the
Teddington Society is displayed (see p.70). There is a collection of earlier artefacts
and copies of local views.

THE TWICKENHAM MUSEUM

25 The Embankment, Twickenham TW1 3DU. Tel 020 8408 0070.
www.twickenham-museum.org.uk/tour.asp. Former 18th century boatman's cottage
maintained by an independent trust. Stores and displays a collection of watercolours,
engravings and photographs of local views and colour reproductions of works by
major artists. Its website has biographies of local artists.

YORK HOUSE

Richmond Road, Twickenham TW1 3AA.
www.richmond.gov.uk/york_house_venue_hire. The 17th century house owned and
maintained by LBRUT displays items from the Borough Art Collection in the Mayor's
parlour.

APPENDIX 5

Further reading

see also works cited in the reference notes

David G. C. Allan, *Some Noble Patriotic Men – and Women: RSA Members and Prize Winners in the Twickenham Area*, BOTLHS *Paper 69* (1994)

David G.C. Allan and John Lawrence Abbott, eds., *The Virtuoso Tribe of Arts and Sciences: Studies in the Work and Membership of the London Society of Arts* (1992)

Anthony Bailey, *Standing in the Sun: the life of J.M.W. Turner* (1997)

Anthony Beckles Willson, *Mr Pope and Others at Cross Deep, Twickenham in the Eighteenth Century* (1996)

Anthony Beckles Willson, *The Church of St Mary the Virgin, Twickenham* (2000)

Kathryn Barron, 'Verrio, Antonio (c.1693-1707)', *Oxford Dictionary of National Biography* (2004)

Cécile Brett, 'Antonio Verrio: his career and surviving work', *British Art Journal*, Winter 2009/10, pp.4-17

Morris K. Brownell, *Alexander Pope and the Arts of Georgian England* (1978)

T.H.R. Cashmore, D.H. Simpson and A.C.B. Urwin, *Alexander Pope's Twickenham – 18th Century Views of his 'Classic Village'*, BOTLHS *Occasional Paper 3* (1988)

T.H.R. Cashmore, *The Orleans Family in Twickenham 1800-1932*, BOTLHS *Paper 49* (1982, 1989, 1997)

E. Croft-Murray, *Decorative Painting in England 1537-1837*, Vol.1 (1962)

Mark de Novellis, *Highlights of the Richmond Borough Art Collections: Orleans House Gallery, Twickenham* (2002)

Mark de Novellis, *Orleans House* (2009)

J.H. Francis and A.C.B. Urwin, *Francis Francis (1822-1886): angling and fishing culture in Twickenham, Teddington and Hampton*, BOTLHS *Paper 65* (1991)

Bamber Gascoigne and Jonathan Ditchburn, *Images of Twickenham with Hampton and Teddington* (1981)

Garth Groombridge, *Teddington, Twickenham and Hampton Past and Present* (2007)

G.D. Heath, *The Chapel Royal at Hampton Court*, BOTLHS *Paper 42* (1979)

Ken Howe and John Sheaf, *Hampton and Teddington Past* (1995)

Ken Howe, Mike Cherry and John Sheaf, *Twickenham, Teddington and Hampton in Old Photographs* (1996, 1998)

Andrew Holt, *Teddington: a history and celebration* (2005)

Christopher Lloyd, *Andrea Mantegna: the Triumphs of Caesar* (1991)

Christopher Lloyd, *The Queen's Pictures: Royal Collections through the centuries* (1991)

Catherine Parry-Wingfield, *A Brief Account of Sandycombe Lodge: the Twickenham home of J.M.W. Turner RA* (2001)

B.L. Pearce, *Virginia Woolf and the Bloomsbury Group in Twickenham*, BOTLHS *Paper 87* (2007)

C.W.Radcliffe, *Middlesex* (1939)

Donald Simpson, *A Victorian Diarist at York House: Sir Mountstuart Elphinstone Grant Duff 1877-1898*, BOTLHS *Paper 1* (1965)

Donald Simpson, *Twickenham Past: a visual history of Twickenham and Whitton* (1993, 2010)

Michael Snodin, *Strawberry Hill and Horace Walpole.* Paul Mellon Centre for Studies in British Art (2010)

J.D. Stewart, *Sir Godfrey Kneller and the English baroque portrait* (1983)

Simon Thurley, *Hampton Court: a social and architectural history.* Paul Mellon Centre for Studies in British Art (2010)

A.C.B. Urwin, *The Manor House, Twickenham*, BOTLHS *Paper 60* (1987)

Clive Wainwright, *Horace Walpole and his collection* in BOTLHS *Paper 74* (1997)

Denys J. Wilcox, *Margaret Geddes: a retrospective* (1998)

Andrew Wilton, *The Life and Work of J.M.W. Turner* (1979)

Acknowledgements

To Mike Cherry, Chairman of the BOTLHS Publications Committee I owe the idea of attempting to treat the artists of the Twickenham area in the manner used by Brian Pearce for the poets in *The Fashioned Reed*. Mike, his committee, and other Society members have continued with their support throughout the project, and though it might seem unnecessary to repeat names which are also acknowledged in the notes, the following have been of especial help: Anthony Beckles Willson, T.H.R. Cashmore, Paddy Ching, Ian Franklin, Ed Harris, Joan Heath, Ken Howe, R.S. Knight and J.C. Sheaf.

In her preamble to the Epilogue, Mary Eighteen writes of the involvement of the RUTC students, and to her and to Diana Yates and to Peter Moore I give the warmest thanks. Peter Moore's designs for the layout of the book show the skills long familiar to me in his work for the RSA. At the RSA I have received help from Rob Baker, RSA Head of Archives and Library, and Rebecca Short, Archive and Records Management trainee. Susan Bennett, who has either typed or computerised my various books and articles since she first came to the RSA in 1973, and now is a freelance researcher and Honorary Secretary of the William Shipley Group for RSA History, has again given me the utmost support.

Nicholas Cambridge, Chair of the WSG, initiated me into the mysteries of the 'memory stick' which he kindly provided, and Doug Craik, a Trustee of FORCE (Friends of the River Crane Environment), collated the illustrations and drew the maps. Pat Francis, WSG member and, like Doug, a Heathfield South neighbour, proofread the text.

Many 'fugitive' items owe their inclusion to that tireless bibliophile Ronald Sim, and I would have got nowhere in my investigations of the Thames Valley Arts Club without the help of its Chairman, Michael Hart. Michael is of course himself an artist, as is Peter Sanderson, a great nephew of the Club's founder. Other living artists who gave me help are Mutalib Man, Paula Nightingale, Jill Storey and Avril Vellacott. More will be found about them in the text and notes.

These notes also record my debt to Carolyne Blore, Cécile Brett, John Cloake, Michael Snodin and the following institutions and their curatorial staff: The Courtauld Institute of Art (The Witt Librarian); Hampton Court Palace (Chris Stevens); the LBRUT Reference and Lending Libraries and the Local Studies Room (Jane Baxter); the London Borough of Hounslow Local Studies Library (James Marshall); The Orleans House Gallery (Mark de Novellis); The Society of Antiquaries (Adrian James).

I acknowledge with thanks the generous permissions, courtesies and facilities which have been extended by the following institutions, organisations, collections and individuals in the origination, reproduction and sourcing of illustrations: The Royal Collection, H M Queen Elizabeth II, pp.22, 26; The Trustees of the British Museum, p.42; The Tate Gallery, pp.35, 39, 48; Wallraf-Richartz Museum, Cologne, p.60; TfL London's Transport Museum, p.73; Hampton Court Photographic Collection, pp.19, 29; Lewis Walpole Collection, Yale University, pp.33, 41; South Bank Centre Archive, p.74, Richmond Borough Art Collection, Orleans House Gallery, pp.34, 35, 36, 37, 41, 51, 52, 56, 57, 58, 75; Richmond Borough Local Studies Collection, p.76; London Borough of Hounslow Local Studies Collection, p.68; RSA Archives, p.78; Richmond upon Thames College and students past and present, pp.78, 82, 83, 84, 85, 86; Thames Valley Arts Club, p.65; His Grace the Duke of Northumberland, pp.14, 26, 45; The Burghley House Collection, p. 27; the family of the late Eric Fraser, pp.46, 71, 72, 73; Mr Mutalib Man, pp.79, 80; Mr Peter Moore, pp.32, 70, 72; Ms Paula Nightingale, p.60; Mrs Margaret Pearce, pp.7, 75; Mr Ronald Sim, pp. 61, 67; Mr A.J. Stirling, p.53; Mrs Jill Storey, p.69; Ms Avril Vellacott, p.72.

Permission was sought but remained untraced in the case of several images.

D.G.C. Allan
Heathfield South
Twickenham
October 2010

Index

BOROUGH OF TWICKENHAM LOCAL HISTORY SOCIETY

The Society was formed in 1962 to promote interest in, and record the history of, Twickenham, Teddington, Whitton and the Hamptons. We meet for illustrated talks on the first Monday of the month from October to May in St Mary's Church Hall, Church Street, Twickenham at 8pm. Our newsletter is published three times a year with numerous articles of local historical interest and we have visits to places of interest locally and further afield.

The Society is a prolific publisher of historical research papers with over 90 titles many of which are still in print.

Recent titles include:

Horace Walpole and the Berry Sisters. Paper no 89. John Beardmore. £3.

The Highways and Byways of Hampton. A short history of every street in Hampton. Paper no 88. John Sheaf. £3.50

Virginia Woolf and the Bloomsbury Group in Twickenham. Paper no 87. Brian Louis Pearce. £3.50

Hampton 1915-1937. Paper no 86. John Sheaf. £3.50

The Bronze Age Barrow at Teddington. Paper no 85. Ken Howe. £3.

Stephen Hales DD FRS 1677-1761 – Science, Philanthropy and Religion in 18th century Teddington. Paper no 83. Dr David G C Allan. £5.

Louis Kyezor 'The King of Whitton' c1796-1869. Paper no 82. Harold Pollins and Vic Rosewarne. £4.50

For details of all our publications please visit our website at www.botlhs.co.uk.

Membership information is available from the
Membership Secretary, 87 Fifth Cross Road, Twickenham TW2 5LJ.